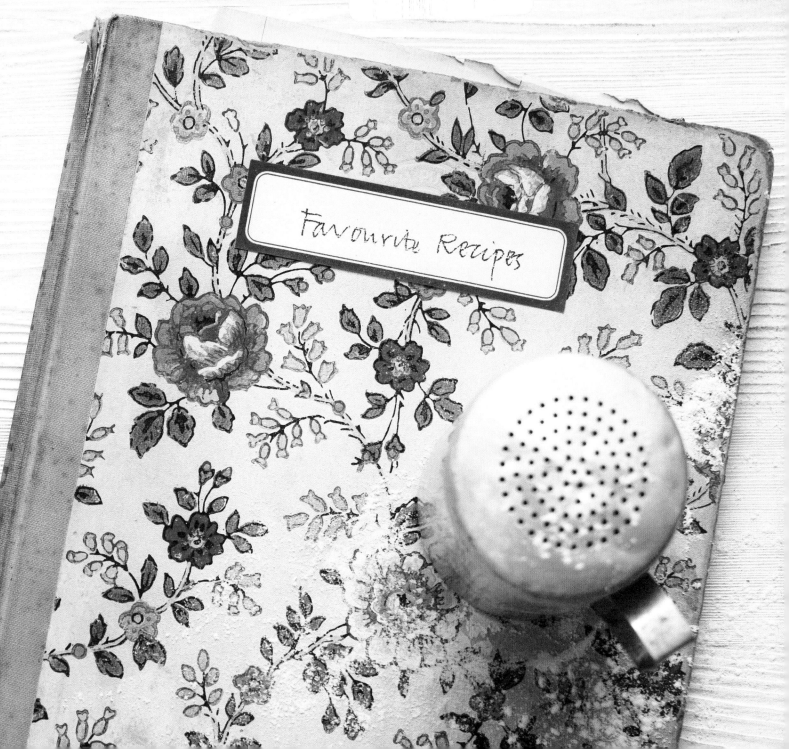

Favourite Recipes

First published in Great Britain
by Simon & Schuster UK Ltd, 2013
A CBS Company

Copyright © WI Enterprises 2013

Recipes previously published in *Homemade Soups*,
One-Pot Dishes and *Traditional Favourites*, 2012

Simon & Schuster Illustrated Books
Simon & Schuster UK Ltd
222 Gray's Inn Road
London WC1X 8HB
www.simonandschuster.co.uk

Simon & Schuster Australia, Sydney
Simon & Schuster India, New Delhi

10 9 8 7 6 5 4 3 2 1

Design: **Richard Proctor**
Photography: **William Shaw**
Stylist and Art Direction: **Tony Hutchinson**
Home Economy: **Sara Lewis**

Colour reproduction by **Dot Gradations Ltd, UK**
Printed and bound in China

A CIP catalogue record for this book is available
from the British Library

ISBN 978-1-47113-256-8

Notes on the recipes

Both metric and imperial measurements have been
given in all recipes. Use one set of measurements
only and not a mixture of both. Spoon measures
are level and 1 tablespoon = 15 ml, 1 teaspoon
= 5 ml.

Preheat ovens before use and cook on the centre
shelf unless cooking more than one item. If using
a fan oven, reduce the heat by 10–20°C, but
check with your handbook.

Medium eggs have been used unless otherwise
stated. This book contains some recipes made
with raw or lightly cooked eggs. Pregnant or
breast-feeding women, invalids, the elderly and
very young children should avoid these dishes.
Once prepared, keep refrigerated.

This book contains recipes made with nuts. Those
with known allergic reactions to nuts and nut
derivatives, pregnant and breast-feeding women
and very young children should avoid these dishes.

The Women's Institute

theWI
INSPIRING WOMEN

comfort food

SIMON &
SCHUSTER
ILLUSTRATED

London · New York · Sydney · Toronto · New Delhi

A CBS COMPANY

Contents

Traditional Favourites

Vegetable stock

You can use whatever vegetables you have to make this stock, adding any herbs that you are fond of.

**Makes about
1.1 litres (2 pints)
Preparation time:
15 minutes
Cooking time:
30–40 minutes
Freezing:
recommended**

1 small **lemon**, scrubbed
and chopped roughly
1 thick **celery stick**,
chopped
2 **carrots**, peeled and
chopped
1 **onion**, chopped
1 teaspoon whole **black
peppercorns**
fresh **herbs** (e.g. parsley
stalks, small bay leaf
and thyme sprig) or
½ teaspoon dried **thyme**
1 small **garlic clove**, sliced
(optional)

Put everything into a large lidded pan with 1.1 litres (2 pints) of water. Bring to the boil, reduce the heat and leave to simmer for 30–40 minutes with the lid of the pan at an angle. This prevents the stock from boiling over and also helps to reduce the volume and increase the flavour. Any scum that rises to the surface should be skimmed off and discarded.

Strain the stock through a fine sieve and taste. You may wish to reduce it further to strengthen the flavour. If necessary, simmer in an open pan until you are happy with the taste.

Tip Use for soups or sauces or freeze for future use. Remember to label carefully, stating the type of stock and date. Only season the stock when you use it.

Chicken stock

Chicken is probably the most useful stock. Freeze the carcasses until you have enough to make a batch. You can also include skin and jelly.

**Makes about
1.1 litres (2 pints)
Preparation time:
10 minutes
Cooking time:
2–2½ hours
Freezing:
recommended**

2 large **chicken carcasses**
or 3 smaller ones
1 large **onion**, sliced
2 **celery sticks**, chopped
1 large **carrot**, peeled and
chopped
fresh **herbs** (e.g. parsley
stalks, small bay leaf,
thyme sprig and tarragon
sprig) or ½ teaspoon dried
tarragon
1 fat **garlic clove**, chopped
(optional)
10 whole **black peppercorns**

Put everything into a large lidded pan (break the carcasses up a bit to fit) with 1.1 litres (2 pints) of water. Bring to the boil, reduce the heat and leave to simmer for 2–2½ hours with the lid of the pan at an angle. This prevents the stock from boiling over and also helps to reduce the volume and increase the flavour. Refrain from boiling hard as this can make the stock cloudy. Any scum that rises to the surface should be skimmed off and discarded.

Strain the stock through a fine sieve and taste. You may wish to reduce it further to strengthen the flavour. If necessary, simmer in an open pan until you are happy with the taste.

Tips Use for soups or sauces or freeze for future use. Before freezing, remove any fat that rises to the surface during cooling. Remember to label carefully, stating the type of stock and date. Only season the stock when you use it.

The colour of this stock is quite light. To make a darker stock, first fry the broken carcasses in oil until they are brown. You can also sear the onion by cutting it in two and frying the cut sides until almost burnt. The resulting stock will be much darker after this treatment. The addition of a glass of dry white wine or even brandy gives another dimension to the flavour. Tarragon is one of Grace's favourite herbs for adding to this stock.

Fish stock

This is very quick to make. You can save white fish bones in the freezer or ask your fishmonger for some. Dry white wine gives it a lovely flavour.

**Makes about
1.1 litres (2 pints)
Preparation time:
10 minutes
Cooking time:
25 minutes
Freezing:
recommended**

900 g (2 lb) **white fish bones**, rinsed
250 ml (9 fl oz) **dry white wine**
115 g (4¼ oz) **white button mushrooms**, sliced
1 small **onion**, sliced
fresh **herbs** (e.g. parsley stalks and tarragon leaves)
5–6 whole **black peppercorns**

Put everything into a large lidded pan with 1.7 litres (3 pints) of water. Bring to the boil, reduce the heat and leave to simmer gently for 20 minutes with the lid of the pan at an angle. This prevents the stock from boiling over and also helps to reduce the volume and increase the flavour. Any scum that rises to the surface should be skimmed off and discarded.

Strain the stock through a fine sieve and taste. You may wish to reduce it further to strengthen the flavour. If necessary, simmer in an open pan until you are happy with the taste.

Tip Use for soups or sauces or freeze for future use. Remember to label carefully, stating the type of stock and date. Only season the stock when you use it.

Beef stock

Store the bones from your Sunday roasts in the freezer and, when you have enough, roast them again in the oven along with some vegetables.

**Makes about
1.1 litres (2 pints)
Preparation time:
15 minutes
Cooking time:
3¼ hours
Freezing:
recommended**

1.3 kg (3 lb) **beef bones** from cooked joints
2 **onions**, topped, tailed and quartered (remove and reserve the skin)
2–3 **celery sticks**, chopped
2 large **carrots**, peeled and chopped
10 whole **black peppercorns**
fresh **herbs** (e.g. parsley stalks, small bay leaf and thyme sprig) or ½ teaspoon dried **thyme**
125 ml (4 fl oz) **red wine** (optional)

First of all, turn the oven to its highest setting. Pack the bones into a large roasting tin, push the onions, celery and carrots in among the bones and roast for about 45 minutes, by which time the bones should have darkened and the vegetables will have softened and scorched just a little.

Transfer the contents of the roasting tin into a large lidded saucepan. Add the onion skins, peppercorns, herbs and 1.7 litres (3 pints) of water. Add the red wine, if using, or a glass of water to the roasting tin and stir vigorously to deglaze the tin and pick up all the flavour. Add the liquid to the saucepan.

Bring to the boil, reduce the heat and leave to simmer for about 2½ hours with the lid of the pan at an angle. This prevents the stock from boiling over and also helps to reduce the volume and increase the flavour. Any scum that rises to the surface should be skimmed off and discarded.

Strain the stock through a fine sieve and taste. You may wish to reduce it further to strengthen the flavour. If necessary, simmer in an open pan until you are happy with the taste.

Tips Meat stock needs to be dark in colour. Use for soups or sauces or freeze for future use. Before freezing, remove any fat that rises to the surface during cooling. Remember to label carefully, stating the type of stock and date. Only season the stock when you use it.

A fair substitute for homemade beef stock is a can of beef consommé, which you can dilute a bit to extend it.

Scallop chowder

The name 'chowder' comes from the French *chaudière*, a large cooking pan. Use any combination of available fish and vegetables to suit your taste.

Serves 4
Preparation time:
  30 minutes
Cooking time:
  15–20 minutes
Freezing:
  not recommended

125 g (4½ oz) rindless
  streaky bacon, chopped
1 large **onion**, chopped
350 g (12 oz) **potatoes**,
  peeled and chopped
1 **carrot**, peeled and
  chopped
1 small **parsnip**, peeled and
  chopped
425 ml (15 fl oz) **fish stock**
  (see page 10)
8 **scallops**
juice of a **lemon**
25 g (1 oz) **plain flour**
600 ml (20 fl oz)
  semi-skimmed milk
salt and freshly ground
  black pepper
1 tablespoon chopped fresh
  parsley, to garnish

Heat a large lidded saucepan and dry fry the bacon over a low heat until the fat is released. Add the onion and sweat, covered, shaking the pan from time to time, until softened but not browned.

Add the remaining vegetables and the stock. Bring to the boil and then reduce the heat and simmer for 15–20 minutes, or until the vegetables are cooked.

Meanwhile, wash the scallops and set the corals aside. Roughly chop the white flesh and sprinkle with the lemon juice.

Blend the flour with a little of the milk until smooth. Add the remainder of the milk and then pour the mixture into the vegetables. Stir until the soup has thickened.

Add the chopped scallops and simmer for 5 minutes. Add the corals and simmer for 2 minutes. Taste and adjust the seasoning if necessary. Serve sprinkled with the parsley.

Butternut squash & apple

Butternut squash is available from autumn through to spring. The combination of flavours makes a delicious soup.

Serves 4
Preparation time:
 25 minutes
Cooking time:
 15–20 minutes
Freezing:
 recommended

1 tablespoon **vegetable** or **olive oil**
1 **onion**, sliced thinly
1 teaspoon **curry powder**
2 **eating apples**, peeled, cored and chopped
1 **butternut squash**, peeled, de-seeded and chopped
1 litre (1¾ pints) **vegetable stock** (see page 8)
salt and freshly ground **black pepper**
Croûtons, to garnish (see page 24)

Heat the oil in a large lidded saucepan. Add the onion and sweat, covered, for 4–5 minutes, shaking the pan from time to time, until softened but not browned.

Stir in the curry powder and apple and cook for 2 minutes.

Add the squash and stock. Bring to the boil and then reduce the heat. Simmer for 15–20 minutes.

Remove the soup from the heat and leave to cool briefly. Blend until smooth. Adjust the seasoning if necessary and then reheat gently. Thin the soup with a little more stock, if wished. Serve scattered with the croûtons.

Cauliflower & broccoli

The addition of walnuts gives this cheesy vegetable soup an interesting crunchy texture.

Serves 4
Preparation and
** cooking time:**
** 25 minutes**
Freezing:
** recommended, before**
** adding cheeses**

1 tablespoon **sunflower oil**
1 small **onion**, chopped
350 g (12 oz) **cauliflower**
  florets
350 g (12 oz) **broccoli florets**
1.1 litres (2 pints) **vegetable**
  stock (see page 8)
25 g (1 oz) **plain flour**
30 ml (1 fl oz) **semi-skimmed**
  milk
25 g (1 oz) **walnuts**,
  chopped
½ teaspoon freshly grated
  nutmeg
200 g (7 oz) **cream cheese**
115 g (4¼ oz) **mature**
  Cheddar cheese, grated
salt and freshly ground
  black pepper
Croûtons, to serve (see
  page 24)

Heat the oil in a large lidded saucepan. Add the onion and sweat, covered, shaking the pan from time to time, until softened but not browned.

Add the cauliflower, broccoli and stock. Cook for 5–10 minutes; the cauliflower and broccoli should be tender but not soft.

Blend the flour and milk together and add to the cauliflower and broccoli. Add the walnuts and nutmeg.

Add the two cheeses and stir the soup over a gentle heat until the cheese is well blended and the soup has thickened. Adjust the seasoning. Serve scattered with the croûtons.

Celery, apple & Stilton

The sharpness of the apple counteracts the richness of the cheese in this unusual soup.

Serves 4
Preparation time:
  20 minutes
Cooking time:
  20 minutes
Freezing:
  recommended, before adding cheese

25 g (1 oz) **butter**
1 **onion**, chopped
3 **celery sticks**, chopped
1 tablespoon **plain flour**
600 ml (20 fl oz) **vegetable stock** (see page 8)
150 ml (5 fl oz) **white wine**
300 ml (10 fl oz) **semi-skimmed milk**
1 **bay leaf**
½ teaspoon dried **mixed herbs**
1 **cooking apple**, peeled, cored and chopped
80 g (3 oz) **Stilton cheese**, diced finely
salt and freshly ground **black pepper**
Croûtons (see page 24), to serve

Melt the butter in a large lidded saucepan. Add the onion and celery and sweat for 2–3 minutes, covered, shaking the pan from time to time, until softened but not browned.

Stir in the flour and cook for a further minute. Gradually add the stock and wine. Bring to the boil, stirring, until thickened.

Add the milk, bay leaf, herbs and apple. Bring back to the boil, cover and simmer for 20 minutes.

Remove the soup from the heat and leave to cool briefly. Remove the bay leaf and blend the soup until smooth.

Add the cheese and heat gently until the cheese has melted. Adjust the seasoning if necessary. Serve scattered with the croûtons.

Red pepper & goat's cheese

This creamy soup is a delicious blend of flavours enriched by the addition of goat's cheese. Everyone who's tried it agrees that it is moreish.

Serves 6
Preparation time:
  20 minutes
Cooking time:
  20 minutes
Freezing:
  recommended, before adding cheese

2 **onions**, chopped
1.7 litres (3 pints) **vegetable stock** (see page 8)
60 ml (2½ fl oz) **dry white wine**
8 **red peppers**, de-seeded and chopped
1 large **cooking apple**, cored and chopped
1 teaspoon chopped fresh **basil**, plus 12 tiny leaves, to garnish
salt and freshly ground **black pepper**
150 g (5½ oz) **goat's cheese**, rind removed, diced
olive oil, to garnish

In a large saucepan, boil the onions in a little of the stock until the stock has evaporated and the onions are beginning to caramelise.

Add the remaining stock, wine, peppers, apple and chopped basil. Cook over a low heat for 20 minutes.

Remove the soup from the heat and leave to cool briefly. Blend until smooth. Adjust the seasoning if necessary and then reheat gently. Add half of the cheese and whisk over a gentle heat until blended.

Serve garnished with the remaining cheese, tiny basil leaves, a drizzle of olive oil and a grinding of black pepper.

Chicken & barley broth

Barley has long been included in traditional soups. It gives great texture and is, happily, making something of a comeback.

Serves 4
Preparation time:
  20 minutes
Cooking time:
  2 hours
Freezing:
  not recommended

1 tablespoon **vegetable**
  or **olive oil**
4 **chicken drumsticks**
1 **onion**, chopped finely
1 **carrot**, peeled and
  chopped finely
1 **celery stick**, chopped
  finely
2 **potatoes**, peeled and
  chopped finely
1 **leek**, sliced finely,
  white and green parts
  separated
1.1 litres (2 pints) **chicken
  stock** (see page 9)
40 g (1½ oz) **pearl barley**
1 **bay leaf**
1 fresh **thyme sprig**
4 tablespoons chopped
  fresh **parsley**
salt and freshly ground
  black pepper

Using a large lidded saucepan, heat the oil over a high heat and fry the drumsticks until they are well browned all over. Use tongs to remove the chicken to a plate and set aside. Lower the heat a little.

Add the onion, carrot, celery, potatoes and white part of the leek to the pan and sweat the vegetables for about 10 minutes, covered, shaking the pan from time to time until the vegetables are softened but not browned (you may need to add a little more oil).

Add the stock, pearl barley, herbs and chicken. Bring to the boil and then reduce the heat to a simmer. Cook for about 2 hours, stirring often. Add the green part of the leek for the last 5 minutes of cooking time (this helps to preserve the green colour).

Remove the chicken to a plate and fish out the bay leaf and thyme sprig. When the chicken is cool enough to handle, separate the meat from the skin and bones. Chop the meat and return it to the broth. Adjust the seasoning and serve.

Curried coconut vegetable

Do not be put off by the list of ingredients in this soup – it is so unusual and delicious that it is worth making the effort!

Serves 6–8
Preparation and cooking time: 1 hour
Freezing: recommended

50 g (1¾ oz) **butter**
seeds from 3 green **cardamom pods** (see Tip)
1 teaspoon **ground coriander**
1 teaspoon **ground cumin**
a large pinch of **turmeric**
2 large **carrots**, peeled and chopped
2 **leeks**, chopped
225 g (8 oz) **celeriac**, peeled and chopped, or 4 thick **celery sticks**, chopped
3 thick **lemongrass stems**, chopped
1 fat **garlic clove**, grated coarsely
2.5 cm (1 inch) fresh **root ginger**, grated
400 ml can **coconut milk**
1.1 litres (2 pints) **chicken stock** (see page 9)
salt and freshly ground **black pepper**

Melt the butter in a large lidded saucepan and fry the cardamom seeds, coriander, cumin and turmeric. Keep the heat low.

Add all the vegetables, lemongrass, garlic and ginger and stir well. Cover and sweat them for a few minutes, shaking often.

Stir in the coconut milk and stock. Bring to the boil and then reduce the heat and leave to simmer for about 30 minutes or until the vegetables are soft.

Blend until smooth and then pour through a nylon sieve into a clean pan. Adjust the seasoning if necessary and then reheat gently. Serve.

Tip To prepare the cardamom pods, roughly crush with the end of a rolling pin or with a pestle and mortar and extract the seeds. Discard the pods.

Green pea, ham & leek

This is a substantial, satisfying soup with a very good flavour and is ideal for lunch on a cold day.

Serves 4
Preparation time:
 25 minutes
Cooking time:
 15 minutes
Freezing:
 **recommended, before
 adding ham**

1 tablespoon **vegetable
 or olive oil**
3 **leeks**, sliced
175 g (6 oz) **frozen peas**
850 ml (1½ pints) **chicken
 stock** (see page 9)
175 g (6 oz) **ham**, cut into
 chunks
2 tablespoons chopped
 fresh **mint**
150 ml (5 fl oz) **double
 cream**, to serve

Heat the oil in a large lidded saucepan. Add the leeks and sweat for 8 minutes, covered, shaking the pan from time to time, until softened but not browned.

Add the peas and stock and bring to the boil. Cover and simmer for 15 minutes.

Remove the soup from the heat and leave to cool briefly. Blend until coarse. Stir in the ham and mint and reheat gently. Serve garnished with a swirl of cream.

Tip For extra taste, use a thick slice of the best quality ham you can get.

Cream of mushroom

This is a classic cream of mushroom recipe with the addition of tasty little croûtons to give it a crunch.

Serves 4
Preparation and
** cooking time:**
** 40 minutes**
Freezing:
** recommended**

50 g (1¾ oz) **butter**
450 g (1 lb) **mushrooms,**
  chopped finely
1 **onion**, chopped finely
1 **garlic clove**, crushed
  (optional)
25 g (1 oz) **plain flour**
450 ml (16 fl oz)
  semi-skimmed milk
450 ml (16 fl oz) **vegetable**
  or **chicken stock** (see
  pages 8 or 9)
salt and freshly ground
  black pepper
150 ml (5 fl oz) **double cream**

Croûtons
(optional)
olive oil
1 thick slice day-old **white**
  bread, crusts removed,
  cubed

Melt the butter in a large lidded saucepan. Add the mushrooms, onion and garlic, if using, and sweat, covered, shaking the pan from time to time, until softened but not browned. Remove a few of the mushrooms and reserve for the garnish.

Add the flour and stir in well. Cook briefly. Add the milk and stock and stir well to make sure the flour is completely blended. Bring to the boil and simmer for 15 minutes.

Meanwhile, make the croûtons. Heat the olive oil and fry the cubes of bread over a brisk heat for a few minutes until browned on all sides. Remove with a slotted spoon and place on kitchen towel to dry. Keep warm.

Remove the soup from the heat and leave to cool briefly. Blend until smooth. Adjust the seasoning if necessary and then reheat gently.

Serve garnished with a swirl of cream, the reserved mushrooms, a grinding of black pepper and the croûtons, if using.

Tip For an extra garnish, fry some sliced chestnut mushrooms in a little butter.

Salmon & dill

This is a lovely soup for a special occasion – rich and creamy and one to impress your friends.

Serves 4–5
Preparation time:
  10 minutes
Cooking time:
  10 minutes
Freezing:
  not recommended

25 g (1 oz) **butter**
1 **onion**, chopped
50 g (1¾ oz) **plain flou**r
700 ml (1¼ pints) **fish stock**
  (see page 10)
450 g (1 lb) **tomatoes**,
  skinned and chopped
  roughly, or 400 g can
  chopped tomatoes
2 x 150 g (5½ oz) **salmon**
  fillets
1 tablespoon chopped fresh
  dill, plus extra sprigs, to
  garnish
2 teaspoons **lemon juice**
150 ml (5 fl oz) **double cream**
80 ml (3 fl oz) **white wine**
salt and freshly ground
  black pepper
curls of zest from ½ a **lemon**

Melt the butter in a large lidded saucepan. Add the onion and sweat for 5 minutes, covered, shaking the pan from time to time, until softened but not browned.

Add the flour and cook, stirring, for a further minute. Stir in the fish stock, making sure the flour is well blended.

Add the tomatoes and salmon. Bring to the boil, cover and simmer for 10 minutes.

Lift the salmon from the pan, remove the skin and flake the flesh, discarding any bones. Set aside.

Remove the soup from the heat and leave to cool briefly. Blend until smooth. Add the dill, lemon juice, cream and wine. Adjust the seasoning if necessary and then reheat gently.

Serve in shallow bowls, topped with the flaked salmon and garnished with the sprigs of dill, lemon zest and a grinding of black pepper.

Borscht

Borscht is originally from the Ukraine, but it has become popular in many Eastern and Central European countries and right around the world.

Serves **4**
Preparation time:
  15 minutes
Cooking time:
  45–60 minutes
Freezing:
  recommended

1 large **onion**, grated
1 large **potato**, peeled and
  grated
450 g (1 lb) raw **beetroot**,
  peeled and grated
300 ml (10 fl oz) **tomato juice**
600 ml (20 fl oz) **vegetable**
  stock (see page 8) or
  water
1 teaspoon **caraway seeds**
salt and freshly ground
  black pepper
a little freshly grated
  nutmeg

To garnish
150 g (5½ oz) **crème fraîche**
  or **natural yogurt**
snipped fresh **dill**

Put all the vegetables in a large lidded saucepan and add the tomato juice, stock or water and caraway seeds. Bring to the boil, cover and simmer for 45–60 minutes. Season to taste with salt, pepper and nutmeg.

Serve as a coarsely textured soup or cool briefly and then blend until smooth.

Serve hot or cold, garnished with a generous spoonful of crème fraîche or yogurt, a little dill and a grinding of black pepper.

Leek, potato & lavender

Flowers and herbs give soups a unique flavour – lavender has been used in cooking for many years. It is fairly pungent, so do not use too much.

Serves 4–6
Preparation time:
  30 minutes
Cooking time:
  30 minutes
Freezing:
  recommended

1 tablespoon **vegetable** or
  olive oil
2 **leeks**, chopped, white and
  green parts separated
450 g (1 lb) **potatoes**, peeled
  and chopped
850 ml (1½ pints) **vegetable
  stock** (see page 8)
300 ml (10 fl oz)
  semi-skimmed milk
6 **lavender sprigs**, tied in
  a piece of muslin, plus
  a few petals, to garnish
salt and freshly ground
  black pepper
4–6 tablespoons **crème
  fraîche**, to serve

Heat the oil in a large lidded saucepan. Add the white parts of the leeks and sweat, covered, shaking the pan from time to time, until softened but not browned. Add the potatoes and stir thoroughly.

Add the stock, milk and lavender flowers. Bring to the boil, cover and simmer for about 30 minutes or until the vegetables are tender. Add the green parts of the leeks for the last 10 minutes of cooking.

Remove the soup from the heat and leave to cool briefly. Remove the bundle of lavender and then blend until smooth. Adjust the seasoning if necessary and then reheat gently. Serve garnished with a spoonful of crème fraîche and a few lavender petals.

Tarragon chicken

Chicken and tarragon is a classic combination that works perfectly together in this easy summery soup.

Serves 4–5
Preparation and cooking time:
45 minutes
Freezing:
not recommended

25 g (1 oz) **butter**
1 large **onion**, sliced finely
2 tablespoons **plain flour**
850 ml (1½ pints) **chicken stock** (see page 9)
finely grated zest and juice of ½ a **lemon**
225 g (8 oz) cooked, skinless, boneless **chicken**, cubed
1 tablespoon chopped fresh **tarragon**, plus extra sprigs, to garnish
150 ml (5 fl oz) **double cream**
salt and freshly ground **white pepper**

To garnish
finely sliced **lemon zest**
edible flowers (e.g. viola, borage)

Heat the butter in a large lidded saucepan. Add the onion and sweat for 5 minutes, covered, shaking the pan from time to time, until softened but not browned.

Add the flour and cook for 1 minute, stirring all the time. Gradually add the stock, making sure all the flour is well blended, and bring to the boil, stirring until thickened.

Add the lemon zest and juice, cover and simmer for 10 minutes. Add the chicken and tarragon and simmer for a further 5 minutes.

Remove the soup from the heat and leave to cool briefly. Stir in the cream. Adjust the seasoning if necessary and then reheat gently. Serve garnished with lemon zest and a few edible flowers.

Fish & tomato

Serves 4
Preparation and
cooking time:
40 minutes
Freezing:
recommended

2 **onions**, sliced
1 **leek**, white part only,
   sliced
3 fat **garlic cloves**, crushed
700 ml (1¼ pints) **fish stock**
   (see page 10)
1 **red pepper**, de-seeded
   and chopped
450 g (1 lb) **tomatoes**,
   skinned and chopped
1 tablespoon **tomato purée**
grated zest of ½ a **lemon**
juice of a **lemon**
1 small **cooking apple**,
   peeled, cored and
   chopped
3 tablespoons **dry white**
   wine
1 **bouquet garni** (see Tip)
450 g (1 lb) **white fish**, cut
   into bite-sized pieces
salt and freshly ground
   black pepper
3 tablespoons chopped
   fresh **parsley**, to garnish

Soften the onions, leek and garlic in a little of the stock in a large saucepan over a medium heat for 10 minutes.

Add the remaining stock, pepper, tomatoes, tomato purée, lemon zest and juice, apple and wine. Drop in the bouquet garni. Bring to the boil, reduce the heat and simmer for 10 minutes.

Remove the bouquet garni. Add the fish and gently simmer for 5 minutes. Adjust the seasoning if necessary. Serve scattered with the parsley.

Tip You can make your own bouquet garni of 1 fresh thyme sprig, 1 fresh marjoram sprig and 3 fresh parsley sprigs, tied with string or white cotton.

Broad bean

Provided broad beans are eaten young they have a delicate flavour. They freeze well and are delicious with ham or bacon, hence this soup.

Serves 4
Preparation time:
   20 minutes
Cooking time:
   15 minutes
Freezing:
   recommended

25 g (1 oz) **butter**
1 **onion**, chopped
225 g (8 oz) podded and
   shelled fresh **broad beans**
175 g (6 oz) shelled fresh
   peas
425 ml (15 fl oz) **vegetable
   stock** (see page 8)
115 g (4¼ oz) lean **bacon**,
   chopped
300 ml (10 fl oz)
   semi-skimmed milk
salt and freshly ground
   black pepper

Melt the butter in a large lidded saucepan. Add the onion and sweat, covered, shaking the pan from time to time, until softened but not browned.

Add the beans, peas and stock, with half the bacon, and bring to the boil. Reduce the heat and simmer for 15 minutes, or until the vegetables are tender.

Meanwhile, dry fry the remaining bacon in a non-stick pan until crispy.

Remove the soup from the heat and leave to cool briefly. Blend half the soup until smooth and then return to the pan with the unblended soup. Add the milk and mix well. Adjust the seasoning if necessary and then reheat gently. Serve garnished with the crispy bacon.

Tip If fresh broad beans and peas are not in season, use frozen.

Lamb & leek

This is a modern version of Scotch broth or Welsh cawl. Use whatever vegetables you have at hand.

Serves 4
Preparation and cooking time: 1 hour
Freezing: recommended

25 g (1 oz) **butter**
225 g (8 oz) **neck fillet of lamb**, cubed
1 large **onion**, chopped
450 g (1 lb) mixed **root vegetables** (e.g. carrots, swede and parsnip), chopped
1.1 litres (2 pints) **chicken stock** (see page 9)
1 **potato**, peeled and chopped
225 g (8 oz) **leeks**, sliced
salt and freshly ground **black pepper**
juice of ½ a **lemon**, to taste
2 tablespoons chopped fresh **mint** or **parsley**

Melt the butter in a large lidded saucepan and sauté the lamb cubes until slightly brown. Remove from the pan.

Add the onion to the same pan and sweat for 5 minutes, covered, shaking the pan from time to time, until softened but not browned.

Return the lamb to the pan with the root vegetables. Add the stock, bring to the boil and simmer for 15 minutes.

Add the potato and simmer for a further 10 minutes. Add the leeks and simmer for a further 5–10 minutes.

Adjust the seasoning if necessary and add lemon juice to taste. Add the mint or parsley, reserving a little to sprinkle on top. Serve at once, sprinkled with the reserved chopped mint or parsley.

Roasted root vegetable

Roasting vegetables is well worth the effort as it gives the soup a different flavour. Vary the vegetables according to your taste and what is available.

Serves 6
Preparation time:
 35 minutes +
 30 minutes
 marinating
Cooking time: 1 hour
Freezing:
 recommended

450 g (1 lb) **celeriac**, peeled
 and cut into wedges
1 large **parsnip**, peeled and
 quartered lengthways
2 **carrots**, peeled and halved
 lengthways
8 **shallots**
1 large **sweet potato**,
 peeled and cut into eight
3 tablespoons **olive oil**
1 tablespoon fresh **thyme**
 leaves
salt and freshly **ground**
 pepper
850 ml (1½ pints) **vegetable**
 stock (see page 8)
6 tablespoons **single cream**
 or **natural yogurt**, to serve
 (optional)

Place all the vegetables in a large roasting tin, toss with the oil and sprinkle with the thyme and seasoning. Set aside to marinate for at least 30 minutes. Preheat the oven to 230°C/450°F/Gas Mark 8.

Roast the vegetables for 45 minutes, until the vegetables are beginning to brown.

Transfer to a large saucepan. Add the stock, bring to the boil and simmer for 15 minutes or until the vegetables are tender.

Remove the soup from the heat and leave to cool briefly. Blend until smooth, adding a little extra stock if necessary. Adjust the seasoning if necessary and then reheat gently.

Serve garnished with a swirl of cream or yogurt, if using.

Chilli bean

Feel free to add a little more or less chilli powder to suit your taste, and don't forget that the sausage will add spice too.

Serves 4–6
Preparation time:
  30 minutes
Cooking time:
  20 minutes
Freezing:
  recommended,
  without the sausage

1 tablespoon **vegetable**
  or **olive oil**
1 large **onion**, chopped
2 **carrots**, peeled and diced
425 g can **kidney beans**,
  drained and rinsed
1 teaspoon **chilli powder**
400 g carton **chopped**
  tomatoes
1 tablespoon **tomato purée**
600 ml (20 fl oz) **chicken**
  stock (see page 9)
salt and freshly ground
  black pepper
sliced **spicy sausage**, such
  as chorizo (optional)

Heat the oil in a large lidded saucepan. Add the onion and carrot and sweat, covered, shaking the pan from time to time, until softened but not browned.

Add the kidney beans and chilli powder. Cook for 1 minute. Add the tomatoes, tomato purée, stock and seasoning. Bring to the boil, reduce the heat, cover and simmer for 20 minutes.

Meanwhile, dry fry the sausage slices, if using, in a small non-stick pan until cooked.

Remove the soup from the heat and leave to cool briefly. Blend half the soup until coarsely chopped. Return to the remaining soup in the pan and reheat gently. Serve garnished with a few small slices of spicy sausage, if using.

Courgette & feta

Another great recipe to use up the late summer glut of courgettes. Teaming them with feta adds a lovely tanginess.

Serves 4
Preparation time:
 30 minutes
Cooking time:
 15–20 minutes
Freezing:
 recommended

2 tablespoons **olive oil**

1 large **onion**, chopped

2 **garlic cloves**, crushed

450 g (1 lb) **courgettes**, sliced

225 g (8 oz) **potatoes**, peeled and chopped

1 teaspoon chopped fresh **parsley**, plus extra, to garnish

700 ml (1¼ pints) **vegetable stock** (see page 8)

80 g (3 oz) **feta cheese**

salt and freshly ground **black pepper**

Heat the oil in a large lidded saucepan. Add the onion and garlic and sweat, covered, shaking the pan from time to time, until softened but not browned. Add the courgettes and potatoes and sweat for about 10 minutes.

Add the parsley and stock, bring to the boil and cook for 15–20 minutes or until the vegetables are softened.

Remove the soup from the heat and leave to cool briefly. Blend until smooth. Add the feta and, off the heat, stir until melted. Adjust the seasoning if necessary and then reheat gently. Serve scattered with the extra parsley.

Butterbean & celeriac

Butterbeans give this soup a creamy texture and complement the taste of the celeriac beautifully.

Serves 4
Preparation time:
  20 minutes +
  12 hours soaking
Cooking time:
  1¾ hours
Freezing:
  recommended

225 g (8 oz) dried
  butterbeans
1 litre (1¾ pints) **vegetable
  stock** (see page 8)
2 **onions**, chopped
1 **celeriac**, peeled and
  chopped
1 teaspoon **caraway seeds**
2 tablespoons chopped
  fresh **parsley**
600 ml (20 fl oz)
  semi-skimmed milk
salt and freshly ground
  black pepper

Place the butterbeans in a large bowl, cover with water and leave to soak for 12 hours.

Drain the beans, rinse well and transfer to a large saucepan. Pour in the stock, bring to the boil and cook for 1 hour.

Add the onions, celeriac, caraway seeds and parsley and simmer until the beans are tender (about another 45 minutes).

Remove the soup from the heat and leave to cool briefly. Blend until smooth and add the milk. Adjust the seasoning if necessary and then reheat gently. Serve.

Curried parsnip

Parsnips work wonderfully in many different soups. This one has just a touch of spice to warm you up on a cold day.

Serves 4
Preparation time:
 30 minutes
Cooking time:
 45 minutes
Freezing:
 recommended

1 tablespoon **vegetable
 or olive oil**
450 g (1 lb) **parsnips**, peeled
 and sliced
1 **onion**, chopped
1 teaspoon **curry powder**
700 ml (1¼ pints) **vegetable
 stock** (see page 8)
150 ml (5 fl oz)
 semi-skimmed milk
salt and freshly ground
 black pepper

To garnish
½ **onion**, sliced
1 tablespoon **olive oil**
4 tablespoons **natural
 yogurt**

Heat the oil in a large lidded saucepan. Add the parsnips and onion and sweat for 10 minutes, covered, shaking the pan from time to time, until softened but not browned.

Add the curry powder and cook for 2–3 minutes. Add the stock and milk and simmer for 45 minutes.

Meanwhile, fry the onion slices in the olive oil until light brown and crispy. Remove with a slotted spoon and set aside on kitchen towel to drain.

Remove the soup from the heat and leave to cool briefly. Blend until smooth. Adjust the seasoning if necessary and then reheat gently. Serve garnished with a spoonful of yogurt and a few crispy onion slices.

Creamy mussel

This is a complete meal in itself. Mussels are plentiful around the coast of north Wales and they are reputed to be some of the finest in this country.

Serves 4
**Preparation and
  cooking time: 1 hour**
**Freezing:
  not recommended**

2 kg (4½ lb) fresh **mussels**
300 ml (10 fl oz) **dry white
  wine**
2 **bay leaves**
6 whole **black peppercorns**
25 g (1 oz) **butter**
1 large **onion**, chopped
4 **garlic cloves**, crushed
300 ml (10 fl oz)
  semi-skimmed milk
salt and freshly ground
  black pepper
150 ml (5 fl oz) **single cream**
2 tablespoons chopped
  fresh **parsley**

Wash the mussels several times to remove any sand. Remove the 'beards' and discard any mussels that are broken or open.

Put the wine, bay leaves and peppercorns in a large lidded saucepan and bring to the boil. Add the mussels, cover and cook on a high heat for 3–4 minutes, shaking the pan to ensure all the mussels cook.

Discard any mussels that have not opened. Drain and reserve the liquor and remove most of the mussels from their shells, setting a few in their shells aside for garnish. Keep warm.

Melt the butter in the pan, add the onion and garlic and sweat, covered, shaking the pan from time to time, until softened but not browned.

Add the strained mussel liquor and the milk. Bring to the boil and then reduce the heat and leave to simmer until the onions and garlic are cooked. Adjust the seasoning if necessary.

Add the mussels, cream and parsley and reheat gently. Serve immediately, garnished with the reserved mussels in their shells.

Pumpkin & apple

This recipe works with any kind of pumpkin and is a lovely orange colour. It originally came from Australia, where pumpkins are used a lot for soup.

Serves 7–8
Preparation time:
  45 minutes
Cooking time:
  45 minutes
Freezing:
  recommended

80 g (3 oz) **butter**

2 large **onions**, sliced

1 kg (2 lb 4 oz) peeled and de-seeded **pumpkin flesh**, chopped

1 large **carrot**, peeled and chopped

1 large ripe **tomato**, chopped

1 **Granny Smith** or small **cooking apple**, peeled, cored and chopped

½ teaspoon **salt**

½ teaspoon **curry powder**

1.1 litres (2 pints) **vegetable stock** (see page 8)

freshly ground **black pepper**

3 tablespoons chopped fresh **mint**, to garnish

Melt the butter in a very large lidded saucepan, add the onions and sweat for at least 10 minutes, covered, shaking the pan from time to time, until softened but not browned.

Add everything else except the mint and stir well. Bring to the boil and then reduce the heat and leave to simmer for about 45 minutes or until all the vegetables are soft.

Remove the soup from the heat and leave to cool briefly. Blend until smooth (you will have to do this in batches). If the purée is too thick, add a little more water. Adjust the seasoning if necessary and then reheat gently. Serve scattered with the mint.

Split pea & ham

Peas and ham go beautifully together and this is an old favourite, enhanced by the addition of a little nutmeg.

Serves 4
Preparation time:
 45 minutes
Cooking time:
 45 minutes
Freezing:
 recommended

1 tablespoon **vegetable** or **olive oil**
1 large **onion**, chopped
1 **garlic clove**, crushed or chopped
a little freshly grated **nutmeg**
175 g (6 oz) **gammon**, chopped finely
175 g (6 oz) **dried split peas**
850 ml (1½ pints) **vegetable** or **chicken stock** (see pages 8 or 9)
½ teaspoon **caster sugar**
150 ml (5 fl oz) **single cream**
salt and freshly ground **black pepper**
chopped fresh **parsley**, to garnish

Heat the oil in a large lidded saucepan. Add the onion and garlic and sweat for 5 minutes, covered, shaking the pan from time to time, until softened but not browned.

Add the nutmeg and gammon and cook for a further 5 minutes.

Add the peas and stock. Bring to the boil, cover and simmer for 45 minutes or until the peas are mushy.

Stir in the sugar and cream and reheat gently. Adjust the seasoning if necessary. Serve sprinkled with the parsley.

Sweet potato & orange

This soup is refreshing, slightly sweet and a delightful colour; it's the ideal remedy for jaded appetites.

Serves 4
Preparation and cooking time:
  20 minutes
Freezing:
  recommended

25 g (1 oz) **butter**
1 **onion**, chopped
450 g (1 lb) **sweet potatoes**, peeled and grated
2 **celery sticks**, very finely chopped
850 ml (1½ pints) **vegetable stock** (see page 8)
2 fresh **thyme sprigs**
grated zest and juice of an **orange**
1 tablespoon chopped fresh **parsley**
salt and freshly ground **black pepper**

Melt the butter in a large lidded saucepan. Add the onion and sweat, covered, shaking the pan from time to time, until softened but not browned.

Add the sweet potatoes, celery, stock, thyme sprigs and orange zest. Bring to the boil and simmer for 10 minutes.

Remove the thyme sprigs and stir in the orange juice and parsley. Adjust the seasoning and then reheat gently if necessary. Serve.

Artichoke & spinach

This soup is made with knobbly Jerusalem artichokes. Don't miss out the hazelnuts – they are perfect with the soup.

Serves 4–5
Preparation time:
   45 minutes
Cooking time:
   20–25 minutes
Freezing:
   recommended

40 g (1½ oz) **butter**
1 small **onion**, sliced finely
350 g (12 oz) **Jerusalem artichokes**, peeled and sliced finely
600 ml (20 fl oz) **chicken stock** (see page 9)
175 g (6 oz) young **spinach leaves**, washed and tough stems discarded
salt and freshly ground **black pepper**
a little freshly grated **nutmeg**
300 ml (10 fl oz) **semi-skimmed milk**
80 g (3 oz) whole skinned **hazelnuts**, toasted, if wished, and slivered (see Tip), to garnish

Melt the butter in a large lidded saucepan. Add the onion and sweat, covered, shaking the pan from time to time, until softened but not browned.

Stir in the artichokes. Continue to sweat the vegetables for about 10 minutes.

Pour in the stock and bring to the boil. Reduce the heat and simmer gently, stirring often, for about 20–25 minutes or until the artichokes are really soft.

Add the spinach to the soup and remove the pan from the hob. (The spinach cooks enough in the residual heat of the pan and thus retains its colour.)

Leave to cool briefly and then blend until smooth. Adjust the seasoning if necessary and add a little grated nutmeg to taste. Stir in the milk and then reheat gently, without boiling. Serve garnished with the slivered hazelnuts.

Tip The best way to sliver the hazelnuts is with a slicing disc on a food processor.

French onion

Serves 6
Preparation and cooking time:
   2½ hours
Freezing:
   recommended, without the croûtes

115 g (4¼ oz) **butter**
2 kg (4 lb 8 oz) large **onions**, sliced as thinly as possible, slices cut into short lengths
1 tablespoon **plain flour**
1.5 litres (2¾ pints) best quality rich and jellied **beef stock**
150 ml (5 fl oz) **dry white wine**
a splash of **brandy** or **Calvados**
salt and freshly ground **black pepper**

Croûtes
1 **garlic clove**, crushed
1 teaspoon chopped fresh **parsley**
50 g (1¾ oz) **butter**, softened
1 small **baguette**, cut into 2.5 cm (1 inch) thick slices
175 g (6 oz) **Gruyère cheese**, grated finely

Melt the butter in a large lidded saucepan and add the onions. Stir well and then turn the heat to the lowest setting and cover the onions with a circle of dampened greaseproof paper. Allow the onions to soften for about 1 hour, stirring frequently.

Remove the paper and turn up the heat. Stir constantly and allow the onions to brown evenly.

Sprinkle the flour over the onions and stir and cook for a couple of minutes. Add the stock, a little at a time, stirring without stopping. As the soup thickens, add the wine and a splash of brandy or Calvados. Simmer for about 1 hour and adjust the seasoning if necessary. Preheat the oven to 220°C/425°F/Gas Mark 7.

To make the croûtes, add the garlic and parsley to the butter and beat well. Spread the slices of bread with the garlic butter and dip each buttered side into the grated cheese. Set the bread slices, cheesy-side up, on a baking sheet. Bake for about 10–15 minutes or until the cheese is bubbly and golden. Leave the bread to cool. If you wish, break the slices into bite-sized pieces. (This makes it much easier to eat.)

Warm six fairly large ovenproof soup bowls. Check that the soup is very hot and then divide it between the bowls. Place the cheesy toasts on the surface and sprinkle over the rest of the cheese. Place the bowls under a grill or in the oven and bake or grill until the cheese melts and bubbles. Serve at once.

Stilton & pear

This delicious recipe was given to us by farmer's wife, Liz Pexton. She and her husband have a farm near Driffield in East Yorkshire.

Serves 4
**Preparation and
  cooking time: 1 hour**
**Freezing:
  recommended**

15 g (½ oz) **butter**
1 **onion**, finely chopped
4 ripe **pears**, peeled, cored
  and chopped
850 ml (1½ pints) **chicken
  stock** (see page 9)
115 g (4¼ oz) **Stilton cheese**,
  crumbled
juice of ½ a **lemon**
salt and freshly ground
  black pepper
snipped fresh **chives**,
  to garnish

Melt the butter in a large lidded saucepan. Add the onion slowly and sweat, covered, shaking the pan from time to time, until softened but not browned.

Add the pears and stock. Simmer until the pears are tender (simmering time will depend on the type and ripeness of the pears).

Remove the soup from the heat and leave to cool briefly. Blend until smooth and then reheat gently.

Add the crumbled Stilton and stir until it melts. Add the lemon juice to taste and adjust the seasoning if necessary. Serve scattered with the snipped chives.

Carrot & coriander

A classic combination of flavours, this soup could also be cooked in the microwave (see Tip).

Serves 4
Preparation time:
 15 minutes
Cooking time:
 15 minutes
Freezing:
 recommended

25 g (1 oz) **butter**
1 **onion**, chopped
1 **garlic clove**, crushed
25 g (1 oz) **plain flour**
1 litre (1¾ pints) **chicken stock** (see page 9)
450 g (1 lb) **carrots**, peeled and grated
2 teaspoons chopped fresh **coriander**
salt and freshly ground **black pepper**
4 tablespoons **natural yogurt**, to serve

Melt the butter in a large lidded saucepan. Add the onion and garlic and sweat, covered, shaking the pan from time to time, until softened but not browned.

Blend in the flour and then add the stock gradually, stirring all the time over a low heat.

Add the carrots and coriander. Bring the soup to the boil and then let it simmer for 15 minutes.

Remove the pan from the heat and adjust the seasoning if necessary. Serve garnished with a swirl of yogurt.

Tip The general method for cooking soup in the microwave is to melt the butter first and then soften the onions in the butter on full power for 4 minutes. Allow another 4 minutes to sauté the vegetables. Add half the recommended quantity of boiling stock to the vegetables and cook on full power for 5 minutes. Stir and cook for a further 5 minutes or until the vegetables are cooked. Add the remaining boiling stock and continue as for conventional cooking.

Jerusalem artichoke

This soup is nearly saffron coloured, due to the carrots. It looks and tastes delicious and few people can guess what's in it.

Serves 4
Preparation time:
  10 minutes
Cooking time:
  30 minutes
Freezing:
  recommended

25 g (1 oz) **butter**
1 **onion**, chopped
2 **celery** sticks, chopped
1 litre (1¾ pints) **vegetable stock** (see page 8)
350 g (12 oz) **Jerusalem artichokes**, peeled and chopped
225 g (8 oz) **carrots**, peeled and chopped
salt and freshly ground **black pepper**

Melt the butter in a large lidded saucepan. Add the onion and celery and sweat for 5 minutes, covered, shaking the pan from time to time, until softened but not browned.

Add the stock and simmer for 20 minutes. Add the artichokes and carrots and cook for a further 10 minutes.

Remove the soup from the heat and leave to cool briefly. Blend until smooth. Adjust the seasoning if necessary and then reheat gently. Serve.

Tip Jerusalem artichokes discolour quickly so, as you peel each one, put it in a bowl of cold, salted water to keep the pale colour.

Beef with dumplings

Serves **4**
Preparation and
  cooking time:
  60–75 minutes
Freezing:
  **recommended,
  without dumplings**

40 g (1½ oz) **butter**
400 g (14 oz) **stewing beef**,
  trimmed of fat and cubed
1 **onion**, chopped finely
1 litre (1¾ pints) **beef stock**
  (see page 11)
450 g (1 lb) mixed **root
  vegetables**, peeled and
  chopped
1 **leek**, sliced thinly
2 tablespoons chopped
  fresh **parsley**
salt and freshly ground
  black pepper

Dumplings
50 g (1¾ oz) **self-raising flour**
15 g (½ oz) **suet**
1 teaspoon chopped fresh
  parsley
fresh **thyme** leaves
salt and freshly ground
  black pepper
about 2 teaspoons
  semi-skimmed milk

Melt half the butter in a large lidded saucepan and quickly fry the beef to seal and brown. Remove with a slotted spoon.

Melt the remaining butter, add the onion and fry until golden. Add the stock and return the beef to the pan. Bring to the boil, reduce the heat and leave to simmer for 10 minutes.

Add the mixed root vegetables, bring back to the boil and then leave to simmer until the beef and vegetables are tender, about 35–50 minutes.

Meanwhile, make the dumplings. Mix the flour, suet, herbs and seasoning together in a bowl. Blend together with the milk until you have a soft but not sticky dough. Shape into eight small balls by rolling in floury hands.

Add the leek and parsley to the soup and simmer for a further 5 minutes.

Add the dumplings to the soup and cook for 5 minutes. Turn after 5 minutes and cook for about 5 minutes more. The dumplings should be light and fluffy when cooked.

Adjust the seasoning if necessary and serve piping hot.

Tip Try adding 1–2 teaspoons of English mustard for extra flavour.

Carrot & apple

Carrot is another vegetable that works so well with many other ingredients. This is a beautiful soup that goes down well throughout the year.

Serves 4
Preparation time:
 10 minutes
Cooking time:
 15 minutes
Freezing:
 recommended

1 tablespoon **olive oil**
25 g (1 oz) **butter**
1 **onion**, chopped
450 g (1 lb) **carrots**, peeled and chopped
225 g (8 oz) **apples**, peeled, cored and chopped
875 ml (1½ pints) **vegetable stock** (see page 8)
salt and freshly ground **black pepper**
a little freshly grated **nutmeg**, to serve

Heat the oil and butter in a large lidded saucepan until the butter has melted. Add the onion, carrots and apples and sweat for 5 minutes, covered, shaking the pan from time to time, until softened but not browned.

Add the stock and cook for 15 minutes, or until the vegetables and apples are tender.

Remove the soup from the heat and leave to cool briefly. Blend until smooth. Adjust the seasoning if necessary and then reheat gently. Serve sprinkled with a little nutmeg.

Hearty winter

This is a substantial soup that is simple to make but very tasty. It is also great for using up winter vegetables.

Serves 4
Preparation time:
25 minutes
Cooking time:
30 minutes
Freezing:
recommended

600 ml (20 fl oz) **vegetable** or **chicken stock** (see pages 8 or 9)
1 **potato**, peeled and diced
1 **onion**, diced
1 large **carrot**, peeled and diced
1 **tomato**, skinned and chopped roughly
1 **turnip** or ½ a **swede**, peeled and diced
1 small **parsnip**, peeled and diced
1 tablespoon **tomato purée**
2 tablespoons chopped fresh **parsley**
salt and freshly ground **black pepper**

Put the stock into a large lidded saucepan and bring to the boil. Add the vegetables, together with the tomato purée.

When the stock is just at the boil, reduce the heat, cover and simmer gently for about 30 minutes or until the vegetables are tender. Stir in most of the parsley and adjust the seasoning if necessary.

Serve this soup as it is or remove from the heat, leave to cool briefly and blend until smooth. Reheat gently if necessary and serve scattered with the remaining parsley.

Chicken pesto

This is a substantial soup, which can be served as a main course. It is colourful, satisfying and there is only one pan to wash at the end!

Serves 4–6
Preparation and cooking time:
30 minutes
Freezing:
recommended, without pesto

1 tablespoon **vegetable or olive oil**

2 **chicken leg portions**, halved

1 large **onion**, chopped

2 tablespoons **plain flour**

1 litre (1¾ pints) **chicken stock** (see page 9)

1 tablespoon **tomato purée**

salt and freshly ground **black pepper**

80 g (3 oz) **baby pasta shapes**

225 g (8 oz) **broccoli**, cut into small florets, stalk sliced

115 g (4¼ oz) **French beans**, sliced thickly

2 tablespoons **pesto**, plus extra to serve

Heat the oil in a large saucepan and fry the chicken pieces on both sides until browned, about 10 minutes.

Add the onion and continue to fry for a further 10 minutes, stirring occasionally. Stir in the flour to combine with the juices.

Add the stock and tomato purée and season. Stir well to make sure the flour is completely blended, bring to the boil, cover and simmer for 15 minutes. Stir in the pasta and cook for 5 minutes.

Add the broccoli and French beans and cook for a few more minutes, until the vegetables and pasta are tender but not soft.

Remove the chicken from the pan. When cool enough to handle, discard the skin and bones and cut the meat into thin strips. Return to the pan, together with the pesto.

Stir well, reheat gently and serve, with additional pesto on the side so that your guests can add it to the bowls themselves.

Winter lentil & mint

This is a lovely soup for a cold wintery day, served piping hot. Dried mint loses its flavour quickly, so this recipe uses mint sauce from a jar.

Serves 4–6
Preparation time:
  10 minutes
Cooking time:
  30 minutes
Freezing:
  recommended, before blending

1 tablespoon **vegetable**
  or **olive oil**
a knob of **butter**
1 **onion**, sliced finely
1 small **garlic clove**, sliced
2 tablespoons **tomato purée**
115 g (4¼ oz) **Puy lentils**
1.1 litres (2 pints) **vegetable**
  or **chicken stock** (see
  pages 8 or 9)
40 g (1½ oz) **bulgar wheat**
2 teaspoons **lemon juice**
2 heaped teaspoons **mint**
  sauce or 2 tablespoons
  chopped **fresh mint**
salt and freshly ground
  black pepper

Melt the oil and butter in a large lidded saucepan. Add the onion and garlic and sweat, covered, shaking the pan from time to time, until softened but not browned.

Add the tomato purée and lentils and stir so that all is well mixed. Add the stock and bring to the boil. Reduce the heat and leave to simmer for about 30 minutes, or until the lentils are soft.

Remove the soup from the heat and leave to cool briefly. Blend half the soup until smooth.

Return the blended soup to the pan and stir in the bulgar wheat, lemon juice and mint sauce or fresh mint. Adjust the seasoning if necessary and simmer for another 2 minutes. Serve piping hot.

Chestnut & cranberry

This is a recipe developed to use up Christmas leftovers! Sweet chestnuts and sharp cranberries combine to give a delicious, satisfying soup.

Serves 6
Preparation and
cooking time:
25 minutes
Freezing:
recommended, after
blending

6 **shallots**, chopped
3 **celery sticks**, chopped
1 litre (1¾ pints) **vegetable stock** (see page 8)
a fresh **thyme sprig**, plus a few extra thyme leaves, to garnish
450 g (1 lb) peeled, cooked **chestnuts**
115 g (4¼ oz) fresh **cranberries**
4 tablespoons **port**
2 tablespoons **lemon juice**
salt and freshly ground **black pepper**
150 ml (5 fl oz) **double cream**, to garnish

Put the shallots, celery and 2 tablespoons of stock in a large saucepan and soften the vegetables over a low heat until transparent.

Add the remaining stock and thyme. Bring to the boil, reduce the heat and leave to simmer for 10 minutes. Add the chestnuts and cranberries. Bring to the boil and simmer for a further 5 minutes. Remove 4 tablespoons of drained vegetables, chestnuts and cranberries for the garnish, crumbling any large pieces of chestnut.

Remove the soup from the heat and leave to cool briefly. Blend until smooth. Stir in the port and lemon juice to taste, adjust the seasoning if necessary and then reheat gently.

Serve topped with a swirl of cream, the reserved garnish ingredients and a few thyme leaves.

Tips Make this at any time of year using frozen cranberries and canned or vacuum-packed chestnuts or unsweetened chestnut purée.

To skin fresh chestnuts, puncture each chestnut with a fork, put in a pan of boiling water and keep at simmering point. Remove a few chestnuts at a time and plunge into cold water. Skin with the help of a vegetable knife.

Chick pea & tomato

We all say at one time or another, 'What on earth is there to eat?' This soup is a good answer, as it can be made mostly from store cupboard ingredients.

Serves 4
Preparation time:
   10 minutes
Cooking time:
   30 minutes
Freezing:
   recommended

2 tablespoons **sunflower oil**
1 **red onion**, chopped
2 **garlic cloves**, crushed
2 teaspoons **cumin seeds**
1 teaspoon **mild curry powder**
2 x 400 g cans **chopped tomatoes**
175 g (6 oz) **carrots**, peeled and diced
50 g (1¾ oz) **red lentils**
finely grated zest and juice of an **orange**
425 g can **chick peas**, drained and rinsed
salt and freshly ground **black pepper**
Croûtons, to garnish (see page 24)

Heat the oil in a large lidded saucepan. Add the onion, garlic, cumin seeds and curry powder and sweat for 5 minutes, covered, shaking the pan from time to time, until softened but not browned.

Add the tomatoes, carrots, lentils and orange zest. Make up the orange juice to 600 ml (20 fl oz) with water and stir into the soup. Bring to the boil, cover and simmer for 30 minutes until the carrots are tender.

Remove the soup from the heat and leave to cool briefly. Blend until smooth or use a potato masher to give fairly coarse texture. Add the chick peas and adjust the seasoning if necessary. Reheat gently and serve scattered with the croûtons.

Leek & broccoli

A delicious winter soup that is full of green goodness. It's very quick to make, too – perfect at the end of a busy day.

Serves 4
Preparation time:
 10 minutes
Cooking time:
 15 minutes
Freezing:
 not recommended

50 g (1¾ oz) **butter**
450 g (1 lb) **leeks**, sliced
 thinly
225 g (8 oz) **broccoli**,
 chopped
1 **garlic clove**, crushed
 (optional)
2 tablespoons **plain flour**
600 ml (20 fl oz) **vegetable** or
 chicken stock (see pages
 8 or 9)
600 ml (20 fl oz)
 semi-skimmed milk
salt and freshly ground
 black pepper
4 tablespoons **single cream**
 or **crème fraîche**, to
 garnish

Melt the butter in a large lidded saucepan. Add the leeks, broccoli and garlic (if using) and sweat for 5 minutes, covered, shaking the pan from time to time, until softened but not browned.

Sprinkle in the flour, stir well and cook briefly. Add the stock, make sure all the flour is blended and bring to the boil. Reduce the heat and cook for 15 minutes, or until the vegetables are softened.

Remove the soup from the heat and leave to cool briefly. Blend until smooth if you wish, or leave it chunky. Add the milk, adjust the seasoning if necessary and then reheat gently. Serve garnished with a swirl of cream or crème fraîche.

Vegetable chowder

Chowders are usually made with milk or cream and often contain seafood. Here, we have used winter vegetables for a tasty, satisfying soup.

Serves 4
Preparation and cooking time:
  50 minutes
Freezing:
  recommended

1 tablespoon **vegetable or olive oil**
1 large **onion**, chopped
225 g (8 oz) **potatoes**, peeled and chopped
225 g (8 oz) **carrots**, peeled and diced
3 **celery sticks**, diced
400 g can **chopped tomatoes**
115 g (4¼ oz) **macaroni**
425 ml (15 fl oz) **vegetable stock** (see page 8)
1 **bay leaf**
1 teaspoon dried **oregano**
300 ml (10 fl oz) **semi-skimmed milk**
salt and freshly ground **black pepper**
chopped fresh **parsley**, to garnish

Heat the oil in a large lidded saucepan. Add the onion, potatoes, carrots and celery and sweat for 5 minutes, covered, shaking the pan from time to time, until softened but not browned.

Add the tomatoes, macaroni, stock and herbs. Bring to the boil, reduce the heat, cover and simmer for 15 minutes.

Stir in the milk and adjust the seasoning if necessary. Discard the bay leaf and bring back to the boil. Serve scattered with the parsley.

Sweet potato & red pepper

The pinkish colour of the sweet potato and deep red of the pepper give this soup a delightful colour, and the coconut milk adds a tropical flavour.

Serves 4
Preparation time:
  35 minutes
Cooking time:
  20 minutes
Freezing:
  recommended

25 g (1 oz) **butter**
1 **onion**, chopped
1 **garlic clove**, crushed
1 tablespoon **ground coriander**
450 g (1 lb) **sweet potatoes**, diced, plus extra to garnish
2 **red peppers**, de-seeded and chopped
700 ml (1¼ pints) **vegetable stock** (see page 8)
400 g can **coconut milk**
vegetable oil, for frying

Melt the butter in a large lidded saucepan. Add the onion and garlic and sweat, covered, shaking the pan from time to time, until softened but not browned.

Stir in the ground coriander and cook for 2 minutes. Add the sweet potatoes and red peppers and cook for 5 minutes. Pour the vegetable stock over, bring to the boil, cover and simmer for 20 minutes.

Meanwhile, cut the extra sweet potato into thin slices (use a mandolin if you have one). Heat about 1 cm (½ inch) of vegetable oil in a frying pan and fry the slices in batches until golden and crisp. Remove with a slotted spoon and place on kitchen towel to dry.

Remove the soup from the heat and leave to cool briefly. Blend until smooth. Add the coconut milk and then reheat gently. Serve at once, garnished with the sweet potato crisps.

Tip If you can't find coconut milk, use 100 g (3½ oz) of creamed coconut, chopped, and increase the amount of stock by about 150 ml (5 fl oz).

Cabbage & bacon

This is a modern version of boiled bacon and cabbage, a perennial favourite. It is quick and easy to make, looks good and tastes even better!

Serves 4
**Preparation and
  cooking time:
  20 minutes**
**Freezing:
  recommended**

25 g (1 oz) **butter**
2 **onions**, chopped finely
6 rindless **bacon rashers**,
  chopped
1 litre (1¾ pints) **vegetable
  stock** (see page 8)
450 g (1 lb) **Savoy cabbage**,
  sliced thinly
salt and freshly ground
  black pepper

Melt the butter in a large lidded saucepan. Add the onions and sweat, covered, shaking the pan from time to time, until softened but not browned.

Add the bacon and increase the heat. Stirring continuously, cook until the onions and bacon begin to brown. Add the stock and bring to the boil.

Add the cabbage. Cook until the cabbage is tender but still firm, approximately 5 minutes. Adjust the seasoning if necessary before serving.

Bean with guacamole salsa

Serves 6
Preparation and
cooking time:
50 minutes
Freezing:
recommended,
without salsa

2 tablespoons **vegetable**
   or **olive oil**
2 **onions**, chopped
4 fat **garlic cloves**, crushed
2 teaspoons **ground cumin**
a pinch of **cayenne pepper**
1 tablespoon **paprika**
1 tablespoon **tomato purée**
2 tablespoons **ground**
   coriander
400 g can **chopped**
   tomatoes
400 g can **red kidney beans**,
   drained and rinsed
1 litre (1¾ pints) **vegetable**
   stock (see page 8)
salt and freshly ground
   black pepper

Guacamole salsa
2 **avocados**
1 **green chilli**
1 **red onion**
1 tablespoon chopped fresh
   coriander
juice of a **lime**

Heat the oil in a large lidded saucepan. Add the onions and garlic and sweat, covered, shaking the pan from time to time, until softened but not browned.

Add all the remaining soup ingredients, bring to the boil and simmer over a low heat for 20 minutes.

Meanwhile, peel and stone the avocados and chop the flesh roughly. De-seed and finely chop the chilli and finely chop the onion. Mix all the salsa ingredients together.

Remove the soup from the heat and leave to cool briefly. Blend until smooth. Adjust the seasoning if necessary and then reheat gently.

Serve garnished with a little of the salsa in the middle of each bowl.

Broccoli & Stilton

Perfect for a Boxing Day lunch, this is a great way to use up leftover Stilton, a classic Christmas cheese.

Serves 6
Preparation and cooking time:
50 minutes
Freezing:
not recommended

1 tablespoon **vegetable** or **olive oil**
1 **onion**, chopped
2 large **potatoes**, peeled and chopped
1.1 litres (2 pints) **vegetable** or **chicken stock** (see pages 8 or 9)
350 g (12 oz) **broccoli**, chopped roughly
80 g (3 oz) **Stilton cheese**, crumbled, plus a little extra, to garnish
150 ml (5 fl oz) **semi-skimmed milk**
juice of ½ a **lemon**
salt and freshly ground **black pepper**

Heat the oil in a large lidded saucepan. Add the onion and sweat, covered, shaking the pan from time to time, until softened but not browned.

Add the potatoes and stock and bring to the boil. Simmer for 10 minutes. Add the broccoli and cook for a further 10 minutes.

Remove the soup from the heat and leave to cool briefly. Blend until smooth or just mash the vegetables roughly if you prefer a chunkier texture.

Add the Stilton and milk, and add lemon juice to taste. Adjust the seasoning if necessary and reheat gently. Serve garnished with a little crumbled Stilton.

Scotch broth

Start this recipe the day before you need it, so that you can chill the soup overnight and remove every scrap of fat from the top for the best flavour.

Serves 6
Preparation time:
  20 minutes +
  overnight chilling
Cooking time:
  3 hours 20 minutes
Freezing:
  recommended

900 g (2 lb) **scrag end of lamb**, trimmed of all excess fat
115 g (4¼ oz) **pearl barley**
1 **bouquet garni**
salt and freshly ground **black pepper**
1 **onion**, chopped finely
1 small **white turnip**, peeled and diced
2 large **carrots**, peeled and diced, or 2 tablespoons diced **swede**
115 g (4¼ oz) **cabbage**, shredded
1 large **leek**, sliced
1 tablespoon finely chopped fresh **parsley**, to garnish (optional)

Place the lamb in a large heavy-based saucepan and add the pearl barley, bouquet garni and 2 litres (3½ pints) of water. Season. Bring the pan slowly to the boil. Skim any white scum from the surface, cover and simmer for 2 hours.

Add the onion, turnip and carrot or swede to the soup and continue to simmer for 1 hour.

Remove the lamb from the soup with a slotted spoon and leave it to stand until it is cool enough to handle. Strip the meat from the bones and cut into small pieces. Cover and set aside in the fridge.

Allow the soup to cool and then chill it overnight so that the fat rises and sets on the surface. Remove the fat and then bring the soup back up to the boil.

Return the lamb to the soup and add the cabbage and leek. Top up with extra water if needed. Bring back to the boil, adjust the seasoning if necessary and simmer for another 20 minutes. Serve scattered with the parsley, if using.

Minestrone soup

Serves 4–6
Preparation and cooking time: 55 minutes

1 tablespoon **olive oil**
115 g (4¼ oz) **pancetta** or rindless **back bacon**, snipped into pieces
1 **leek**, finely sliced
1 **carrot**, peeled and diced
1 **celery stick**, finely sliced
1 large **onion**, finely chopped
400 g can **chopped tomatoes**
1.4 litres (2½ pints) good-quality **vegetable**, **ham** or **chicken stock**
1 **bay leaf**
1 tablespoon **tomato purée**
½ x 410 g can **cannellini** or **butter beans**, drained and rinsed
50 g (1¾ oz) small **pasta**
a handful of fresh **basil leaves**, torn
salt and freshly ground **black pepper**
175 g (6 oz) **Savoy cabbage** or **spring greens**, shredded
finely grated **Parmesan cheese**, to garnish (optional)

Heat the oil in a large lidded saucepan. Add the pancetta or bacon, leek, carrot, celery and onion. Toss them in the oil, cover and leave to sweat over a low heat for 10 minutes, without browning. Shake the pan occasionally.

Add the tomatoes, stock, bay leaf and tomato purée. Bring to the boil, cover and simmer for 20 minutes.

Add the beans, pasta and basil. Season and return to the boil. Simmer for another 10 minutes, or until the pasta is cooked.

Three minutes before the end of the cooking time, add the cabbage or spring greens to the pan, cover and allow it to steam on top of the soup. Stir through the cabbage or greens and serve with a bowl of Parmesan, if using, for guests to add themselves.

Tip Minestrone is usually finished off with a generous topping of grated Parmesan. Personally, I feel that this rather 'takes over' from the subtle flavour of the vegetables. As a compromise, hand round a bowl of freshly grated Parmesan for those who feel that the soup needs it.

Variation Vary the vegetables according to the season – for instance, substitute courgettes or spinach for the cabbage during the summer months.

Spiced sweet potato soup

The hint of chilli powder and cumin makes this a warming soup for the cooler days of autumn and winter.

Serves 6
Preparation time: 35 minutes
Cooking time: 20 minutes

1 tablespoon **olive oil**, plus extra to garnish

1 **onion**, chopped

2 **garlic cloves**, crushed

2 **red peppers**, de-seeded and diced

250 g (9 oz) **sweet potato**, peeled and diced

350 g (12 oz) **vine tomatoes**, de-seeded and roughly chopped

a pinch of **chilli powder**

½ teaspoon **ground cumin**

850 ml (1½ pints) **vegetable stock**

½ teaspoon **caster sugar**

freshly ground **black pepper**

fresh **basil leaves**, to garnish (optional)

Heat the olive oil in a large lidded saucepan and gently cook the onion and garlic for 5 minutes until softened but not browned. Stir in the red peppers, sweet potato and tomatoes, along with the chilli powder and cumin. Cook for a further 5 minutes to soften the vegetables.

Pour in the stock, bring up to the boil, reduce the heat and then cover and leave to simmer for 20 minutes until the vegetables are tender.

Allow the soup to cool a little and then, using a blender or food processor, purée the soup in batches until smooth. Pass the soup through a sieve to remove any small pieces of tomato skin and return it to the rinsed-out saucepan. Stir in the sugar and check the seasoning, adding some freshly ground black pepper, if desired.

Gently reheat the soup, then serve immediately in warmed bowls, garnishing with a drizzle of olive oil and fresh basil, if using.

Tip Using vine tomatoes, although slightly more expensive, really enhances the flavour of the soup.

Seriously spicy lentil soup

A wonderfully robust soup based on a traditional Indian dhal. Adjust the quantity of chilli according to your own taste.

Serves 6
Preparation and cooking time:
45 minutes

1 tablespoon **vegetable oil**
1 **onion**, chopped
1 **red pepper**, de-seeded and diced
2 **garlic cloves**, crushed
2.5 cm (1 inch) **fresh root ginger**, finely chopped
½ teaspoon **chilli powder**
½ teaspoon **turmeric**
½ teaspoon **ground coriander**
225 g (8 oz) **split red lentils**
850 ml (1½ pints) **vegetable stock**, plus extra if needed
400 g can **chopped tomatoes**
1 tablespoon **tomato purée**
salt and freshly ground **black pepper**

To garnish
natural **yogurt**
finely chopped fresh **coriander leaves**

Heat the vegetable oil in a large lidded saucepan and gently fry the onion for 3–4 minutes until softened but not coloured. Stir in the pepper and garlic and cook for a further 3–4 minutes.

Add the ginger, chilli powder, turmeric, ground coriander and lentils. Stir well to coat with the oil. Add the vegetable stock, tomatoes and tomato purée, stir and bring up to the boil. Reduce the heat, cover the pan and simmer the soup for 20–25 minutes, stirring occasionally, until the lentils are cooked.

Using a blender or food processor, blend half the soup to give a chunky texture. If you prefer a smoother textured soup, then purée the whole amount. Reheat the soup, adjusting the seasoning to taste and topping up with extra stock if needed to adjust the thickness of the soup. Ladle into warmed bowls and garnish with a swirl of yogurt and chopped coriander.

Tip For an optional garnish, heat 1 tablespoon of sunflower oil in a small non-stick frying pan and fry 1 teaspoon of crushed coriander seeds and ¼ teaspoon of turmeric until golden.

Golden broth

A traditional soup from Northern Ireland thickened with oatmeal and full of delicious vegetables. Serve with some freshly baked wholemeal soda bread.

Serves 4
Preparation time: 20 minutes
Cooking time: 40-45 minutes

25 g (1 oz) **butter**
1 large **onion**, finely chopped
1 **celery stick**, finely chopped
2 **carrots**, peeled and finely chopped
25 g (1 oz) **plain flour**
600 ml (20 fl oz) **chicken stock**, plus extra if needed
300 ml (10 fl oz) **semi-skimmed milk**
25 g (1 oz) medium **oatmeal**
125 g (4½ oz) **spinach**, washed and chopped
freshly ground **black pepper**

Melt the butter in a large lidded saucepan. Add the onion, celery and carrots and cook for 4–5 minutes to just soften the vegetables.

Stir in the flour and cook for a further minute, stirring constantly. Pour in the chicken stock followed by the milk and bring to the boil, stirring, to thicken the soup slightly. Reduce the heat, cover the pan and simmer gently for 30 minutes. Stir occasionally.

Sprinkle the oatmeal over the surface of the soup and stir it in. Add the spinach and stir that in. If necessary, add a little extra stock to reduce the thickness of the soup. Continue to cook gently for a further 10–15 minutes, stirring occasionally to prevent the soup sticking.

Serve the soup immediately in warmed bowls, garnished with a grinding of black pepper.

Tip Don't worry if it looks as if you have too much spinach to fit into the pan, it wilts down very quickly as soon as it touches the liquid.

Italian bean soup

There's a real flavour of the Mediterranean in this filling soup. You could serve it as a main course accompanied by a tomato and olive bread.

Serves 6
Preparation time: 30 minutes
Cooking time: 30 minutes

2 tablespoons **olive oil**
50 g (1¾ oz) **pancetta**, cubed
1 **onion**, chopped
1 **celery stick**, diced
1 **carrot**, peeled and diced
1 **garlic clove**, crushed
½ teaspoon dried **sage**
1 **bay leaf**
400 g can **chopped tomatoes**
1 litre (1¾ pints) **vegetable stock**
400 g can **borlotti beans**, drained and rinsed
400 g can **cannellini beans**, drained and rinsed
100 g (3½ oz) **French beans**, cut into 4 cm (1½ inch) lengths
75 g (2¾ oz) **spaghetti**, broken into short pieces
1 tablespoon chopped fresh **parsley**
freshly ground **black pepper**

Heat the olive oil in a large lidded saucepan. Add the pancetta and fry gently for 2–3 minutes. Stir in the onion, celery, carrot, garlic, sage and bay leaf. Cook gently for a further 4–5 minutes to soften the vegetables.

Stir in the tomatoes and stock. Bring up to the boil, reduce the heat, cover and simmer gently for 15 minutes. Add the borlotti and cannellini beans and simmer for a further 5 minutes. Remove the bay leaf.

Ladle half the soup into a blender or food processor and purée until smooth. Return to the pan containing the remaining soup and add the French beans and spaghetti pieces. Cook for 7–8 minutes until the spaghetti is 'al dente' and the French beans are just tender.

Remove from the heat and stir in the parsley. Season to taste with black pepper if required. Serve immediately.

Sweet potato & onion soup

This velvety smooth soup was inspired by an old Norfolk recipe. The tangy onions complement the rich creaminess of the sweet potatoes.

Serves 4
Preparation time: 15
minutes
Cooking time:
20 minutes

1 tablespoon **olive oil**
2 large **onions**, sliced
500 g (1 lb 2 oz) **sweet**
potatoes, peeled and
roughly chopped
850 ml (1½ pints) **chicken**
or **vegetable stock**
freshly ground **black pepper**

Heat half the oil in a large lidded saucepan and add half the onions. Fry gently until golden and crispy and then remove with a slotted spoon and reserve.

Add the remaining oil and onions to the pan and fry gently until softened. Add the sweet potatoes and half the stock. Bring to the boil, cover and simmer until the vegetables are tender.

Allow the soup to cool a little and then add the remaining stock. Using a blender or food processor, purée the soup in batches until smooth.

Return the soup to the hob and reheat gently. Season to taste with black pepper and serve garnished with the reserved onions and a grinding of black pepper.

Hearty turkey soup

A clever way to use up leftover turkey at Christmas, this soup is great at any time of the year and can also be made using cooked chicken.

Serves 4–6
Preparation time: 35 minutes
Cooking time: 30 minutes

1 tablespoon **sunflower oil**
1 large **onion**, chopped
3 **celery sticks**, chopped
450 g (1 lb) **potatoes**, peeled and diced
675 g (1½ lb) mixed **root vegetables** (e.g. carrot, parsnip, swede or turnip), peeled and diced
1.1 litres (2 pints) **chicken** or **turkey stock**
400 g can **haricot beans**, drained and rinsed
225 g (8 oz) **cooked turkey**, shredded
2–3 tablespoons chopped fresh **parsley**
salt and freshly ground **black pepper**

Heat the oil in a large saucepan and cook the onion until soft. Stir in the celery, potatoes and root vegetables and cook for 5 minutes.

Add the stock and haricot beans, bring to the boil and simmer for 25 minutes or until the vegetables are soft.

Stir in the turkey and parsley and heat through for 5 minutes. Season to taste before serving.

Thai chicken curry

If you can, use galangal and kaffir lime leaves for a truly authentic curry.
Serve with steamed jasmine rice and lime wedges to squeeze over.

Serves 4
Preparation and
** cooking time:**
** 25 minutes**

1 **lemongrass stem**
450 g (1 lb) skinless,
   boneless **chicken breasts**
1 tablespoon **vegetable oil**
1 **red chilli**, de-seeded and
   finely chopped
1 teaspoon grated fresh **root**
   ginger or **galangal**
1 **garlic clove**, crushed
225 g (8 oz) **chestnut**, **oyster**
   or **shiitake mushrooms**,
   stalks removed, halved
a bunch of **spring onions**,
   sliced thinly, 1 reserved
   for garnish
300 ml (10 fl oz) **coconut**
   milk
150 ml (5 fl oz) **chicken stock**
zest of ½ a **lime**, pared in
   thick strips, plus extra
   thin strips to garnish, or
   2 **kaffir lime leaves**
1 rounded tablespoon
   chopped fresh **coriander**
1 tablespoon **soy sauce**

Remove any tough outer leaves from the
lemongrass. Cut the stem into three and
bruise the pieces. Cut the chicken breasts
into bite-sized pieces, about eight each.

Heat the oil in a wok or large frying pan.
Add the lemongrass, chicken, chilli, ginger
or galangal and garlic. Stir fry for 2 minutes
to seal the meat. Stir in the mushrooms and
cook for a further minute.

Add the spring onions, coconut milk, stock,
lime zest or lime leaves, coriander and soy
sauce. Bring to the boil, reduce the heat
and simmer gently for 8 minutes or until
the chicken pieces are cooked.

Remove the lemongrass and lime zest or
leaves. Shred the remaining spring onion
and scatter it over to garnish, together
with thin strips of lime zest.

Chicken with beans

A quick recipe suitable for a midweek evening meal – it only needs to be accompanied by boiled new potatoes and some lightly steamed broccoli.

Serves 4
Preparation time: 15 minutes
Cooking time: 30-35 minutes

1 **onion**, chopped
4 rashers **smoked back bacon**, chopped
1 **garlic clove**, chopped
4 skinless, boneless **chicken breasts**, cubed
400 g can **chopped tomatoes**
1 teaspoon dried **thyme**
1 teaspoon **paprika**
410 g can **cannellini beans**, drained and rinsed
freshly ground **black pepper**
chopped fresh **parsley**, to garnish

Gently fry the onion, bacon and garlic in a large, lidded, non stick pan for 5–6 minutes to soften the onion and cook the bacon. Add the chicken and continue to cook until the chicken is sealed and lightly golden.

Stir in the tomatoes along with the thyme and paprika. Bring up to the boil and then cover and reduce the heat. Simmer for 20–25 minutes, stirring occasionally.

Add the cannellini beans to the pan and stir into the mixture. Cook for a further 10 minutes until the beans are heated through and the chicken cooked. Season to taste with freshly ground black pepper. Serve immediately, sprinkled with some chopped parsley.

Tip Although the excess fat should be removed from the bacon, there should still be sufficient rendered out in the heat of the pan to cook off the onion and garlic – so don't be tempted to add any oil.

Chicken with black pudding

A Scottish version of the favourite English lamb or beef hotpot. To spice up the sauce, finely diced black pudding has been added. Serve with peas.

Serves 4
Preparation time:
  25 minutes
Cooking time:
  1¾ hours

1 tablespoon **sunflower oil**
2 **onions**, thinly sliced
2 tablespoons **plain flour**
salt and freshly ground
  black pepper
8 boneless, skinless
  chicken thighs
40 g (1½ oz) unsalted **butter**
900 g (2 lb) **potatoes**, thinly
  sliced
1 **dessert apple**, cored
  and sliced
110 g (4 oz) **black pudding**,
  diced
450 ml (16 fl oz) **chicken
  stock**

Preheat the oven to 180°C/350°F/Gas Mark 4. Heat the oil in the base of a lidded flameproof and ovenproof casserole dish, add the onions and fry for 5 minutes, stirring until softened. Remove with a slotted spoon and set aside.

Sift the flour into a shallow dish and season. Use to coat the chicken thighs. Melt half the butter in the casserole dish and fry the chicken in batches until golden on both sides. Remove from the dish and reserve with the onions.

Arrange half the potatoes in the base of the dish, top with the chicken, onions, apple and black pudding and then add the remaining potatoes, arranged overlapping on top. Pour over the stock, season and bring to the boil.

Cover with a lid and transfer to the oven for 1¼ hours. Remove the lid, dot with the remaining butter and cook for a further 30 minutes, uncovered, until the potatoes are golden. Spoon into shallow bowls to serve.

Chicken pasta bake

Serves 4
Preparation time:
20 minutes
Cooking time:
1 hour 20 minutes–
1 hour 30 minutes

1 tablespoon **olive oil**

500 g (1lb 2 oz) boneless,
skinless **chicken thighs**,
cubed

1 **onion**, chopped

1 **red pepper**, de-seeded
and diced

1 **orange pepper**, de-seeded
and diced

2 **garlic cloves**, finely
chopped

1 tablespoon **cornflour**

400 g can **chopped
tomatoes**

300 ml (10 fl oz) **chicken
stock**

3 fresh **rosemary sprigs**,
leaves chopped

salt and freshly ground
black pepper

500 g (1 lb 2 oz) fresh **pasta
quills**

a kettle full of **boiling water**

100 g (3 ½ oz) **mascarpone
cheese**

80 g (3 oz) **Parmesan
cheese**, grated

Preheat the oven to 180°C/350°F/Gas Mark 4. Heat the oil in a flameproof and ovenproof casserole dish, add the chicken a few pieces at a time, until all the pieces are in the dish, and then fry for 5 minutes, stirring until evenly browned. Remove with a slotted spoon and set aside on a plate.

Add the onion to the dish and fry for 5 minutes until softened and just beginning to turn golden. Add the peppers and garlic and cook for a few minutes until just beginning to soften.

Mix the cornflour with a little water until a smooth paste forms and then add to the dish with the tomatoes, stock and rosemary. Season, bring to the boil, stirring, and then add the chicken pieces back in. Cover and transfer to the oven to cook for 1 hour.

When the chicken is almost ready, tip the pasta into a large bowl, cover with boiling water and leave to soak for 5 minutes. Drain.

Remove the casserole dish from the oven, stir the mascarpone into the hot chicken mix and then gently fold in the pasta. Sprinkle with the Parmesan and return the dish to the oven, uncovered, for 20–30 minutes until golden.

Chicken in Dijon sauce

This is a simple all-in-one meal that can be prepared in advance and then cooked just before serving. Serve with rice or baked potatoes.

Serves 4
Preparation time:
  20 minutes + 1 hour marinating
Cooking time:
  30–40 minutes

4 boneless, skinless **chicken breasts**
300 ml (10 fl oz) **white wine**
2 tablespoons **Dijon mustard**
3 tablespoons **olive oil**
2 **courgettes**, sliced
4 small **carrots**, peeled and diced
115 g (4¼ oz) **button mushrooms**
2 tablespoons **cornflour**
300 ml (10 fl oz) **chicken stock**

Cut each chicken breast into six slices and place in a shallow dish. Mix together the white wine and Dijon mustard and pour over the chicken. Leave to marinate, covered, in the fridge for at least 1 hour. Preheat the oven to 180°C/350°F/Gas Mark 4.

Heat the oil in a lidded flameproof and ovenproof casserole dish. Remove the chicken from the marinade, add to the casserole dish and brown on all sides (reserve the marinade). Add the courgettes, carrots and mushrooms and cook for 5 minutes.

Mix the cornflour with a little of the stock and add to the dish with the remaining stock and the marinade. Heat gently until the sauce has thickened.

Cover, transfer to the oven and cook for 30–40 minutes until the chicken is cooked right through.

Chicken korma

For the best flavour the chicken is best left to marinate overnight in yogurt, turmeric and garlic. Serve with rice mixed with chopped fresh coriander.

Serves 4
Preparation time:
  20 minutes +
  overnight marinating
Cooking time:
  30 minutes

4 boneless, skinless
  chicken breasts
150 g (5½ oz) natural **yogurt**
2 **garlic cloves**, crushed
2 teaspoons **turmeric**
40 g (1½ oz) unsalted **butter**
1 large **onion**, sliced
5 cm (2 inches) fresh **root
  ginger**, finely diced
1 teaspoon **chilli powder**
1 teaspoon **coriander
  seeds**, crushed
10 whole **cloves**
1 teaspoon **salt**
5 cm (2 inch) **cinnamon
  stick**
1 tablespoon **cornflour**
150 ml (5 fl oz) **single cream**
25 g (1 oz) **unsalted cashew
  nuts**, toasted, to garnish

Score each chicken breast with a sharp knife. In a large bowl, mix together the yogurt, garlic and turmeric. Add the chicken and coat well in the marinade. Cover and leave to marinate overnight in the fridge.

Melt the butter in a large frying pan, add the onion and cook until soft and browned. Stir in the ginger, chilli powder, coriander seeds, cloves, salt and cinnamon stick and cook for 2–3 minutes.

Add the chicken and its marinade and cook on a gentle heat for 20–25 minutes until the chicken is completely cooked. Reduce the heat.

Blend the cornflour and cream together and stir into the chicken. Reheat very gently to prevent the cream from curdling. Sprinkle over the cashew nuts to garnish and serve.

Pot-roast pesto chicken

Sunday lunch needn't mean lots of pans on the hob. Add everything to one pan then cover and roast in the oven – what could be simpler?

Serves 4
Preparation time:
 20 minutes
Cooking time:
 1 hour 55 minutes

1.5 kg (3 lb 2 oz) whole
 chicken
2 **red** or **white onions**,
 cut into wedges
450 g (1 lb) **tomatoes**,
 roughly chopped
6 **garlic cloves**, finely
 chopped
3 tablespoons **pesto**
1 teaspoon **paprika**
salt and freshly ground
 black pepper
600 ml (10 fl oz) hot **chicken
 stock**
550 g (1 lb 3 oz) **butternut
 squash**, peeled, de-seeded
 and cut into wedges
300 g (10½ oz) **courgettes**,
 thickly sliced
1 **red pepper**, de-seeded
 and thickly sliced
1 **yellow pepper**, de-seeded
 and thickly sliced

Preheat the oven to 180°C/350°F/Gas Mark 4. Add the chicken to a large, lidded, flameproof and ovenproof casserole dish or oval covered roaster. Tuck the onions, tomatoes and garlic around the chicken. Spread 2 tablespoons of pesto over the chicken and then sprinkle with the paprika and season. Pour the stock around the chicken. Cover and transfer to the oven to cook for 1¼ hours.

Remove the lid, baste the chicken breast with the stock and then add the remaining vegetables, pressing as many as you can beneath the stock. Cook, uncovered, for 30 minutes.

Remove from the oven, turn the vegetables, baste with the stock and then spread the remaining 1 tablespoon of pesto over the chicken breasts. Cook for 10 more minutes or until the chicken and vegetables are cooked through and the chicken is golden brown.

Lift out the chicken, carve and serve in shallow bowls with the vegetables and the stock ladled over.

Tarragon chicken

Fresh tarragon has a wonderful aniseed flavour, but don't ever use dried tarragon – it tastes dreadful. Serve with new potatoes and a green salad.

Serves 4
Preparation time:
  35 minutes
Cooking time:
  45 minutes

8 skinless **chicken thighs**
125 ml (4 fl oz) **dry white wine**
½ **onion**, finely sliced
25 g (1 oz) fresh **tarragon**, leaves separated from stalks
1 **chicken stock cube**
salt and freshly ground **black pepper**
100 g (3½ oz) **crème fraîche**

Preheat the oven to 190°C/375°F/Gas Mark 5. Put the chicken in a lidded flameproof casserole dish, add the wine, onion, half the tarragon leaves and the tarragon stalks and 125 ml (4 fl oz) of water. Crumble over the stock cube and season.

Cover and cook in the oven for 45 minutes until the chicken is cooked through. Remove the chicken thighs and keep warm.

Boil the stock over a high heat until reduced by half and then remove the tarragon stalks.

Add the crème fraîche (don't worry if it looks curdled) and boil, stirring well until the sauce thickens. Chop the remaining tarragon leaves, add to the dish and check the seasoning. Put the chicken back into the sauce, stir well and serve.

Braised pork with fennel

A simple pork casserole made with just six ingredients, but full of flavour. The fennel adds sweetness. Serve with roasted sweet potatoes.

Serves 4
Preparation time:
25 minutes
Cooking time:
25–30 minutes

2 tablespoons **sunflower oil**
4 x 175–225 g (6–8 oz) **pork steaks**
225 g (8 oz) **fennel bulb**
1 **red pepper**, de-seeded and diced
225 g (8 oz) **mushrooms**, quartered
400 g can **chopped tomatoes**
salt and freshly ground **black pepper**

Preheat the oven to 200°C/400°F/Gas Mark 6. Heat the oil in a lidded flameproof and ovenproof casserole dish and brown the pork steaks on both sides. Remove and set aside.

Thinly slice the fennel and reserve any feathery leaves for garnish. Cook the fennel slices in the casserole dish until softened. Remove and set aside with the pork steaks.

Fry the pepper and mushrooms for about 5 minutes until soft and then stir in the tomatoes and bring to the boil. Season. Return the pork steaks and fennel to the casserole dish, making sure the steaks are covered by the sauce. Cover with the lid.

Cook for 25–30 minutes until the pork is cooked through and the vegetables are tender. Serve garnished with the feathery fennel leaves.

Pork with herby dumplings

This warming casserole is served with light herby dumplings, which are cooked on the top of the dish and absorb lots of the wonderful flavours.

Serves 4
Preparation time: 30 minutes
Cooking time: 1 hour 20 minutes

1 tablespoon **olive oil**
675 g (1½ lb) lean boneless **pork**, cubed
1 **onion**, sliced
2 tablespoons **plain flour**
1 litre (1¾ pints) **dry cider**
2 **carrots**, peeled and chopped
2 **eating apples**, cored and sliced
1 **bouquet garni**
2 tablespoons **Dijon mustard**
2 tablespoons **Worcestershire sauce**
salt and freshly ground **black pepper**

Herby dumplings
115 g (4¼ oz) **self-raising flour**
50 g (1¾ oz) **vegetable suet**
2 tablespoons chopped fresh or 1 teaspoon dried **mixed herbs**

Preheat the oven to 180°C/350°F/Gas Mark 4. Heat the oil in a large, lidded, flameproof and ovenproof casserole dish and fry the pork until browned. Remove with a slotted spoon and set aside. Add the onion and fry for 5 minutes until lightly browned. Stir in the flour and cook for 1 minute and then gradually stir in the cider until smooth.

Return the pork to the pan with the carrots, apples, bouquet garni, Dijon mustard and Worcestershire sauce. Season well. Cover and cook in the oven for 1 hour.

Meanwhile, mix the flour, suet, herbs and seasoning together. Add 3–4 tablespoons of water and mix lightly to a soft dough. Shape into eight balls. Remove the casserole dish from the oven and add the dumplings, spaced slightly apart. Cover and cook for a further 20 minutes until the dumplings are risen and light.

Sweet & sour pork

Making your own sweet and sour sauce is straightforward, delicious, and infinitely preferable to the ready-made alternative.

Serves 4
Preparation time: 10 minutes
Cooking time: 15 minutes

2 tablespoons **sunflower oil**
350 g (12 oz) **pork fillet** or **tenderloin**, sliced into 1 cm (½ inch) medallions, then halved
1 **onion**, roughly chopped
½ **red pepper,** de-seeded and chopped
½ **green pepper**, de-seeded and chopped
225 g can **bamboo shoots**, drained and rinsed
1½ tablespoons **cornflour**

Sauce
3 tablespoons **cider vinegar**
3 tablespoons **soft light brown sugar**
2 tablespoons **soy sauce**
1½ tablespoons **tomato purée**
150 ml (5 fl oz) **pineapple juice**

For the sauce, combine the vinegar, sugar, soy sauce and tomato purée in a small bowl. Make the pineapple juice up to 225 ml (8 fl oz) with water and stir into the mixture.

Heat 1 tablespoon of the oil in a large lidded wok or frying pan. Add the pork and stir fry over a high heat for 1–2 minutes, turning the meat continuously, until browned. Remove from the pan and set aside.

Add the remaining oil to the pan. Stir fry the onion and peppers for 1 minute. Return the pork to the pan and add the sauce and bamboo shoots. Bring to the boil, reduce the heat, cover and simmer for 5 minutes.

Blend the cornflour with 2 tablespoons of water. Remove the lid from the wok or pan, stir in the cornflour mixture and bubble until the mixture thickens. Heat through, stirring all the time, for 1 minute. Serve at once.

Variation Substitute chicken for the pork, if you prefer.

Madeira pork

A creamy sauce flavoured with Madeira and mushrooms – simple but delicious. Serve with carrot and potato mash and your favourite vegetables.

Serves 4
Preparation time: 25 minutes
Cooking time: 20 minutes

2–3 tablespoons **sunflower oil**
1 **onion**, chopped
1 large **yellow pepper**, de-seeded and diced
675 g (1½ lb) **pork fillet**, trimmed of visible fat and cut into 1 cm (½ inch) slices
1 tablespoon **paprika**
1 tablespoon **plain flour**
300 ml (10 fl oz) **stock**
150 ml (5 fl oz) **Madeira**
175 g (6 oz) **button mushrooms**, quartered
1 tablespoon **tomato purée**
salt and freshly ground **black pepper**
150 ml (5 fl oz) **single cream**

Heat the oil in a large lidded frying pan. Add the onion and pepper and cook for 3–4 minutes. Add the pork slices and brown on all sides. Stir in the paprika and flour and cook for 1 minute.

Blend in the stock and Madeira, bring to the boil and reduce the heat to a simmer. Stir in the mushrooms and tomato purée and season. Cover the pan and simmer gently for 20 minutes or until the pork is tender and cooked through.

Stir in the cream, heat gently and serve straight away.

Variation Ruby port can be used in place of the Madeira if you prefer.

Boiled gammon & peas

Soaked yellow split peas are tied in a cloth and simmered in the same pan as a gammon joint for a nostalgic supper. Serve with English mustard.

Serves 4
Preparation time:
25 minutes +
overnight soaking
Cooking time:
1 hour 50 minutes

1.25 kg (2 lb 12 oz) smoked **gammon joint**
250 g (9 oz) dried **yellow split peas**
2 **onions**, quartered
2 **bay leaves**
350 g (12 oz) **carrots**, peeled and cut into large chunks
225 g (8 oz) **turnips**, peeled and quartered or halved
4 **celery sticks**, thickly sliced
5 **cloves**
a few **black peppercorns**, roughly crushed
350 g (12 oz) **potatoes**, peeled and cut into chunks
2 **small leeks**, cut into 2.5 cm (1 inch) lengths
40 g (1½ oz) unsalted **butter**
salt and freshly ground **black pepper**
chopped fresh **parsley**, to garnish

Add the gammon joint and split peas to separate bowls and cover each with cold water. Leave the peas at room temperature but transfer the gammon to the fridge overnight.

The next day, drain the gammon and split peas. Add the gammon, 1 onion, the bay leaves, carrots, turnip, celery, cloves and peppercorns to a large lidded saucepan. Tie the drained split peas, remaining onion and the potatoes in a large piece of muslin or a linen tea cloth. Add to the pan, cover with cold water and bring to the boil.

Boil rapidly for 10 minutes, skimming any froth off the surface if needed. Reduce the heat to a simmer, cover and cook for 1½ hours or until the gammon and split peas are tender. Add the leeks and cook for a further 10 minutes until just tender.

Lift the bag of split peas from the pan, untie the string and tip the peas, potato and onion into a large bowl. Mash with the butter, a little extra pepper and salt to taste. Spoon onto serving plates.

Carve the gammon and add to the plates with the cooked vegetables, some of the broth and a sprinkling of chopped parsley.

Dijonnaise pork

This is based on a wonderful French recipe. Don't be tempted to use English mustard – it's far too fiery and would completely spoil the sauce.

Serves 4
Preparation time: 15 minutes
Cooking time: 20 minutes

1 tablespoon **sunflower oil**
4 large **pork loin chops**, trimmed of visible fat
freshly ground **black pepper**
100 ml (3½ fl oz) **dry white wine**
1 teaspoon dried **thyme**
150 g (5½ oz) **crème fraîche**
1 teaspoon **tomato purée**
1 tablespoon **Dijon mustard**
1 **tomato**, peeled, de-seeded and diced
1 tablespoon chopped fresh **parsley**

Heat the oil in a large frying pan. Season the pork chops with black pepper and add to the pan. Seal quickly on both sides and then reduce the heat. Cook the chops for a further 3 minutes on each side then remove from the pan to a plate. Pour off all the excess fat and wipe out the pan with kitchen towel.

Return the pan to the heat and pour in the wine. Add the thyme and bubble vigorously for 2–3 minutes until the wine is reduced to about one third of its original volume.

Stir in the crème fraîche and tomato purée and then return the pork chops to the pan. Cook the chops for 5–6 minutes over a medium heat until tender, being careful not to overcook them.

Stir in the Dijon mustard, tomato and chopped parsley. Continue to cook for a further 2–3 minutes until heated through. Serve the chops immediately, with the sauce.

Pork & plum casserole

Best cooked in the late summer, do make sure the plums are ripe. Serve with mashed potatoes and green vegetables.

Serves 6
Preparation time:
   35 minutes
Cooking time:
   1½ hours

1 teaspoon **vegetable oil**
1½ teaspoons **Chinese five spice**
1 **red onion**, sliced
1 **onion**, sliced
2 **garlic cloves**, sliced
3 **celery sticks**, sliced
2 teaspoons dried **basil**
675 g (1½ lb) **lean pork**, cubed
300 ml (10 fl oz) **red wine**
450 g (1 lb) ripe **red plums**, quartered and stoned
1 tablespoon **cornflour**
salt and freshly ground **black pepper**
chopped fresh **parsley**, to garnish (optional)

Preheat the oven to 160°C/320°F/Gas Mark 3. Heat the oil in a lidded flameproof and ovenproof casserole dish. Add the Chinese five spice and cook over a gentle heat for 30 seconds. Add both onions and the garlic and stir fry for 2 minutes. Add the celery and stir fry for 1 minute.

Sprinkle on the basil and stir in the pork and wine, with three-quarters of the plums. Bring to the boil, cover, place on a baking sheet and cook for about 1¼ hours, or until the pork is just tender.

Blend the cornflour to a smooth paste with a little cold water. Stir into the casserole, mixing it through all the liquid. Place the remaining plums on top and return to the oven for 15 minutes, or until the plums have heated through. Check the seasoning and garnish with the parsley, if using.

Tip If you prefer, the quantity of wine can be halved and stock used in its place.

Beef in Guinness cobbler

A traditional British stew with an American twist – the meat is topped with a layer of light scones. Serve with a selection of green vegetables.

Serves 4
Preparation time:
 30 minutes
Cooking time:
 1 hour 50 minutes–
 2½ hours

50 g (1¾ oz) **plain flour**
½ teaspoon freshly grated
 nutmeg
salt and freshly ground
 black pepper
675 g (1½ lb) **chuck steak**,
 cut into 2.5 cm (1 inch)
 cubes
3 tablespoons **olive oil**
25 g (1 oz) unsalted **butter**
2 large **onions**, finely sliced
2 **garlic cloves**, crushed
1 teaspoon **brown sugar**
575 ml (19 fl oz) **Guinness**
zest and juice of an **orange**
1 **bay leaf**

Scone topping
225 g (8 oz) **self-raising flour**
a pinch of **salt**
50 g (1¾ oz) unsalted **butter**
7 tablespoons **semi-
 skimmed milk**

Preheat the oven to 180°C/350°F/Gas Mark 4. Sift the flour into a shallow dish and stir in the nutmeg and plenty of seasoning. Coat the meat in the flour.

Heat half the oil and half the butter in a large, lidded, flameproof and ovenproof casserole dish. Add half the meat and fry for 2–3 minutes until evenly browned. Transfer to a plate, add the remaining oil and butter to the casserole and brown the remaining meat. Transfer to the plate.

Put the onions and garlic in the casserole and fry gently for 5 minutes, stirring constantly. Add the sugar and cook over a moderate heat for a further minute, stirring constantly, until the sugar caramelises.

Return the beef to the casserole and pour the Guinness over the top. Add the orange zest and juice and bay leaf and bring to the boil.

Cover and cook for 1½–2 hours, stirring occasionally and adding a little water to the casserole if the liquid becomes too thick.

For the scone topping, sift the flour and salt into a large bowl and rub the butter in until the mixture forms fine breadcrumbs. Add enough milk to form a soft dough. Knead on a lightly floured surface, roll out to 1 cm (½ inch) thick and cut out 8 scones using a 5 cm (2 inch) cutter.

Remove the casserole from the oven, take off the lid and arrange the scones in an overlapping circle around the edge of the dish, with one in the centre. Return the dish, uncovered, to the oven and cook for a further 20–30 minutes or until the scones are well risen and golden brown.

Beef in red wine

This elegant casserole is great for a dinner party. Prepare the day before and keep in the fridge to let the flavours develop. Serve with garlic bread.

Serves 4
Preparation time:
  25 minutes
Cooking time:
  1½ hours

25 g (1 oz) **plain flour**
salt and freshly ground
  black pepper
500 g (1 lb 2 oz) lean
  braising steak, trimmed
  of visible fat and cubed
1 tablespoon **vegetable oil**
1 large **onion**, sliced
2 **garlic cloves**, crushed
2 **carrots**, peeled and sliced
2 **celery sticks**, sliced
300 ml (10 fl oz) **beef stock**
300 ml (10 fl oz) **red wine**
1 teaspoon dried **thyme**
2 **bay leaves**
2 tablespoons **tomato purée**
225 g (8 oz) **button
  mushrooms**, quartered

Preheat the oven to 160°C/320°F/Gas Mark 3. Sift the flour into a shallow dish and season well. Toss the beef in the seasoned flour to coat lightly.

Heat the oil in a large, lidded, flameproof and ovenproof casserole dish and fry off batches of the beef to brown and seal. Using a slotted spoon, transfer the beef to a plate.

Add the onion, garlic, carrots and celery to the casserole and cook gently for 5–6 minutes until softened. Pour in the beef stock and red wine and add the thyme, bay leaves and tomato purée. Stir to mix in the tomato purée and bring the mixture up to the boil.

Return the beef to the casserole dish, cover and cook in the oven for 1¼ hours. Remove the casserole from the oven, stir in the mushrooms and return to the oven for a further 15 minutes or until the beef is very tender. Check the seasoning and serve immediately.

Beef & sweet vegetables

In this recipe, onion is caramelised and several sweet vegetables are included to develop a sweeter flavour. Serve with baked potatoes.

Serves 4
Preparation time:
  1 hour
Cooking time:
  1 hour 35 minutes–
  1 hour 50 minutes

1 **onion**, sliced
200 g (7 oz) **carrots**, peeled
  and chopped
200 g (7 oz) **leeks**, chopped
200 g (7 oz) **parsnips**, peeled
  and chopped
1 **sweet potato**, peeled and
  chopped
225 ml (8 fl oz) **beef stock**
225 ml (8 fl oz) **beer**, **ale**
  or **lager**
450 g (1 lb) **lean casserole
  beef pieces**, trimmed of
  visible fat
1 **bouquet garni**
freshly ground **black pepper**
2 level tablespoons
  cornflour

Put the onion in a large, lidded, flameproof and ovenproof casserole dish, cover with the lid and place over a low heat. Leave to become golden brown and slightly sticky. Check after 15 minutes to ensure the onion is beginning to brown; if not, raise the heat a little. When the onion is cooked and coloured, remove from the dish (this should take about 30 minutes in total). Preheat the oven to 160°C/320°F/Gas Mark 3.

Place all the other vegetables in the casserole dish. Pour over the stock and beer, ale or lager, cover and bring to the boil. Stir well. Add the beef and bouquet garni and season with black pepper. Stir in the reserved onion and cover.

Place on a baking tray and transfer to the oven. Cook for 1¼–1½ hours, or until the meat and vegetables are just tender.

Mix the cornflour to a smooth paste with a little cold water. Remove the casserole from the oven, pour the cornflour paste over and stir, taking care not to break up the vegetables. Replace the lid and return the casserole to the oven for another 20 minutes. Remove the bouquet garni and serve.

Tip Don't be tempted to cook the casserole for longer than the recommended time because really lean cuts of meat toughen very quickly, even in a casserole.

Lamb in mushroom sauce

Here lamb chops in a mushroom sauce are baked in the oven until tender. Serve with brown rice and stir-fried courgettes and peppers.

Serves 4
Preparation time:
 20 minutes
Cooking time:
 1¼–1½ hours

40 g (1½ oz) unsalted **butter**
8 best end of neck **lamb chops**, trimmed of visible fat
1 tablespoon **plain flour**
300 ml (10 fl oz) **lamb stock**
4 tablespoons **redcurrant jelly**
2 tablespoons **Worcestershire sauce**
2 tablespoons freshly squeezed **lemon juice**
a pinch of freshly grated **nutmeg**
salt and freshly ground **black pepper**
225 g (8 oz) **button mushrooms**

Preheat the oven to 160°C/320°F/Gas Mark 3. Melt the butter in a lidded flameproof and ovenproof casserole dish and quickly brown the chops on all sides. Remove to a plate.

Stir the flour into the remaining fat in the dish, blend in the stock and add the redcurrant jelly, Worcestershire sauce, lemon juice and nutmeg. Season and heat until boiling, stirring continuously.

Return the chops to the dish, together with the mushrooms, making sure the sauce covers the lamb. Cover and cook for 1¼–1½ hours or until the chops are tender.

Mediterranean lamb

Reminiscent of Greek holidays – lamb is marinated in a spicy yogurt mixture and then simmered in a tomato sauce. Serve with a green salad.

Serves 4
Preparation time: 20 minutes + at least 1 hour marinating
Cooking time: 50–60 minutes

225 g (8 oz) **Greek yogurt**
zest of a **lemon**
2 **garlic cloves**, crushed
1 teaspoon **ground cumin**
3 tablespoons **olive oil**
salt and freshly ground **black pepper**
675 g (1½ lb) **lamb fillet**, sliced
1 **onion**, thinly sliced
150 ml (5 fl oz) **dry white wine**
1 **lamb stock cube**
400 g can **chopped tomatoes**
1 tablespoon **tomato purée**
1 teaspoon **caster sugar**
2 **bay leaves**
1 tablespoon fresh **oregano**
80 g (3 oz) stoned **black olives**
175 g (6 oz) canned **artichoke hearts**
6 **mint leaves**, finely chopped

Spoon 3 tablespoons of the yogurt into a large bowl and stir in the lemon zest, garlic, ground cumin and 1 tablespoon of olive oil. Season, place the lamb in the marinade and stir to coat well. Place in the fridge for at least 1 hour to marinate.

Heat the remaining oil in a large lidded frying pan and fry the onion over a gentle heat until tender. Add the meat and fry until browned on all surfaces.

Pour the wine into the pan and stir well. crumble over the stock cube and then add the tomatoes, tomato purée, sugar, bay leaves and oregano. Cover the pan and simmer very gently for about 50–60 minutes until the meat is tender.

Stir in the olives and artichoke hearts and cook for 10 minutes. Mix the remaining Greek yogurt with the mint leaves and serve with the lamb.

Greek-style lamb shanks

This is cooked long and slow for meltingly tender lamb that almost falls off the bone. An easy dish to share with friends.

Serves 4
Preparation and cooking time: 3 hours

2 tablespoons **olive oil**
4 x 350 g (12 oz) **lamb shanks**
2 **onions**, roughly chopped
3 **garlic cloves**, finely chopped
2 teaspoons **coriander seeds**, roughly crushed
2 tablespoons **plain flour**
200 ml (7 fl oz) **white wine**
450 ml (16 fl oz) **lamb stock**, plus extra if needed
1 tablespoon thick-set or runny **honey**
1 **lemon**, cut into wedges
2 **bay leaves**
675 g (1½ lb) small **new potatoes**, scrubbed and thickly sliced
salt and freshly ground **black pepper**
80 g (3 oz) **mixed olives** and **sundried tomatoes**
150 g (5½ oz) frozen **green beans**
chopped **fresh parsley**, to garnish

Preheat the oven to 180°C/350°F/Gas Mark 4. Heat the oil in a large, lidded, flameproof and ovenproof casserole dish. Add the lamb, cooking in batches if needed, and fry, turning for about 5 minutes until brown all over. Remove and set aside.

Add the onions to the dish and fry for 5 minutes, stirring until just beginning to brown. Add the garlic and coriander seeds and then stir in the flour. Gradually pour in the wine and stock and bring to the boil. Add the honey, lemon and bay leaves and then the potato slices. Season.

Return the lamb to the dish, cover and transfer to the oven for 2¼ hours.

Remove the dish from the oven, turn the lamb and add the olives and sundried tomatoes and the still frozen beans. Top up with a little extra stock if needed, cover and cook for a further 15 minutes until the beans are hot and the lamb is very tender. Spoon into large shallow bowls and garnish with the chopped parsley.

Spicy meatball stew

A blend of hot and fiery chilli powder and mild and sweet paprika produces a hearty stew. Serve with spaghetti.

Serves 4
Preparation time: 15 minutes
Cooking time: 30 minutes

450 g (1 lb) **lamb mince**
115 g (4¼ oz) fresh **breadcrumbs**
1 **onion**, grated
1 tablespoon **paprika**
1 **garlic clove**, crushed
1 teaspoon **chilli powder**
25 g (1 oz) stoned **black olives**, chopped
1 tablespoon chopped fresh **parsley**, plus extra to garnish
1 **egg**, beaten
1 tablespoon **vegetable oil**
300 ml (10 fl oz) **lamb stock**
400 g can **chopped tomatoes**
2 **courgettes**, chopped
4 **bay leaves**
salt and freshly ground **black pepper**

In a large bowl, mix together the lamb, breadcrumbs, onion, paprika, garlic, chilli powder, olives, parsley and beaten egg. Ensure that the mixture is evenly combined and then shape into 16 even-sized small balls.

Heat the oil in a large frying pan and gently fry the meatballs for 5–10 minutes until they are evenly browned.

Add the stock, tomatoes, courgettes and bay leaves and season. Bring to the boil, reduce the heat to a gentle simmer, cover and cook for 30 minutes. Remove the bay leaves and serve garnished with extra parsley.

Lancashire hotpot

A traditional recipe of layers of lamb, sliced onions and potatoes cooked in a dish. Boiled carrots or mashed swede are ideal accompaniments.

Serves 4
Preparation time:
 20 minutes
Cooking time:
 1 hour 50 minutes–
 2 hours 20 minutes

25 g (1 oz) **plain flour**
salt and freshly ground
 black pepper
675 g (1½ lb) middle or best
 end of neck **lamb chops**,
 trimmed of visible fat
2 large **onions**, sliced
2 **lamb's kidneys**, skinned,
 cored and sliced
675 g (1½ lb) **potatoes**,
 sliced
1 tablespoon chopped fresh
 rosemary
25 g (1 oz) unsalted **butter**,
 melted
425 ml (15 fl oz) **lamb stock**

Preheat the oven to 180°C/350°F/Gas Mark 4. Sift the flour into a shallow dish and season well. Add the chops and turn to coat evenly in the seasoned flour.

Arrange layers of meat, onion, kidney and potato in a large, lidded, ovenproof casserole dish. Sprinkle each layer with a little rosemary and some seasoning and finish with a layer of potatoes.

Brush the top of the potatoes with the melted butter. Pour the stock into the casserole dish and cover it tightly with a lid. Cook for 1½–2 hours, or until the meat is tender.

Remove the lid from the casserole and cook for an extra 20 minutes to brown the potatoes.

Tip If you don't have a lidded casserole dish, use a regular ovenproof dish and cover with foil.

Sausage & lentil casserole

A superior sausage casserole that is good enough to serve at an informal dinner party. Serve with mashed potatoes and steamed Savoy cabbage.

Serves 4
Preparation time: 40 minutes
Cooking time: 35-40 minutes

1 tablespoon **olive oil**
450 g (1 lb) good quality **sausages**
1 **onion**, sliced
2 **garlic cloves**, crushed
1 teaspoon **ground allspice**
½ teaspoon freshly grated **nutmeg**
2 x 400 g cans **chopped tomatoes**
2 fresh **rosemary sprigs**, plus extra chopped leaves to garnish
2 **bay leaves**
200 ml (7 fl oz) **red wine**
100 g (3½ oz) **Puy lentils**

Heat the oil in a large lidded frying pan or flameproof casserole dish and cook the sausages for 5–8 minutes until nicely browned all over. Remove from the pan and set aside.

Add the onion and garlic to the pan and cook gently until the onion is softened. Stir in the allspice and nutmeg and mix well.

Pour in the tomatoes and bring to the boil. Simmer for 4–5 minutes to thicken slightly and then add the rosemary, bay leaves, red wine and Puy lentils. Stir in 200 ml (7 fl oz) of cold water, return the sausages to the pan and bring back up to the boil.

Cover the pan and reduce the heat. Simmer for 35–40 minutes until the lentils are tender. Stir several times during the cooking to prevent the lentils sticking to the base of the pan, and add a little more water if the sauce is becoming too thick. Remove the rosemary sprigs before serving garnished with a little chopped rosemary.

Venison casserole

This rich and tasty dish is also lovely made with fresh chestnuts (see Tip). Serve with mashed potato and a selection of vegetables.

Serves 4–6
Preparation time:
  25 minutes
Cooking time:
  1½–1¾ hours

3 tablespoons **olive oil**
3 **shallots**, finely chopped
½ **onion**, finely chopped
4 rashers unsmoked **streaky bacon**, chopped
3 **celery sticks**, chopped
25 g (1 oz) **plain flour**
salt and freshly ground **black pepper**
675 g (1½ lb) **venison**, diced
425 ml (15 fl oz) **beef stock**
150 ml (5 fl oz) **red wine**
240 g can cooked peeled **chestnuts**
8 **juniper berries**, lightly crushed
3 tablespoons **Grand Marnier**

Preheat the oven to 160°C/320°F/Gas Mark 3. Heat the oil in a large flameproof and ovenproof casserole dish and fry the shallots and onion gently until cooked. Stir in the bacon and celery and cook for 3–4 minutes. Remove to a plate with a slotted spoon and set aside.

Sift the flour into a shallow dish and season well. Add the venison and turn to coat in the seasoned flour. Add to the casserole dish and fry until browned on all surfaces.

Return the onion, bacon and celery mixture to the casserole. Stir in the stock and red wine and bring to the boil. Add the chestnuts, juniper berries and Grand Marnier.

Cover the casserole dish and cook in the oven for 1½–1¾ hours or until the meat is tender.

Tip To prepare fresh chestnuts, make a slit in each one, place in a pan of boiling water and simmer for 10 minutes. Remove a couple at a time and carefully remove the outer and inner skin. If the inner skin remains, place the chestnuts in fresh boiling water and boil for a further 3 minutes, the skin will then rub off easily.

Smoked haddock stew

This is a lovely recipe, halfway between a stew and a soup. It's very nourishing and filling. Serve with crusty bread.

Serves 4
Preparation time: 20 minutes
Cooking time: 20 minutes

225 g (8 oz) smoked **haddock fillet**

300 ml (10 fl oz) **boiling water**

1 tablespoon **sunflower oil**

1 **onion**, finely sliced

2 **celery sticks**, finely chopped

1 **carrot**, peeled and finely sliced

1 **potato**, peeled and finely diced

½ teaspoon **turmeric**

1 fresh **thyme sprig**

2 **bay leaves**

salt and freshly ground **black pepper**

300 ml (10 fl oz) **semi-skimmed milk**

75 g (2¾ oz) frozen **peas**

freshly grated **nutmeg**

Place the haddock in a large but shallow bowl and pour over the boiling water. Leave for 5 minutes and then drain, reserving the liquid.

Heat the oil in a large lidded saucepan and gently fry the onion for 2 minutes. Add the celery, carrot and potato and continue to fry for 2 more minutes.

Add half of the reserved fish liquid, the turmeric, thyme sprig and bay leaves and season. Bring to the boil and simmer very gently with the lid on until the vegetables are soft, about 15 minutes. Add the rest of the fish liquid, the milk and peas and cook for a further 3 minutes.

Gently flake in the fish, taking care to remove any skin and bones. Remove the bay leaves and thyme sprig and grate in a little nutmeg. Check the seasoning before serving.

Cod with bean mash

This is made in a frying pan with a lid. If your pan doesn't have a lid, improvise with a lid from a large saucepan, a baking tray or a piece of foil.

Serves 4
Preparation time: 10 minutes
Cooking time: 25 minutes

25 g (1 oz) unsalted **butter**

1 **leek**, thinly sliced, white and green parts kept separate

2 x 400 g cans **cannellini beans**, drained and rinsed

zest and juice of a **lemon**

450 ml (16 fl oz) **fish stock**

salt and freshly ground **black pepper**

1 teaspoon **wholegrain mustard**

4 smoked **cod loin pieces**, about 675 g (1½ lb) in total

3 tablespoons **crème fraîche**

4 tablespoons roughly chopped fresh **parsley**

Melt the butter in a large, lidded frying pan, add the green parts of the leek and fry gently for 2–3 minutes until just beginning to soften. Remove with a slotted spoon and set aside.

Add the white parts of the leek to the pan and fry for 2–3 minutes until softened. Add the cannellini beans, lemon zest and juice and stock. Season and bring to the boil. Cover and cook for 5 minutes.

Spread the mustard over the pieces of fish and season. Arrange on top of the bean mixture and cook for 8–10 minutes until just cooked and the fish flakes when pressed with a knife. Lift the fish out of the pan with a fish slice and keep hot on a plate.

Mash the beans coarsely and then stir in the softened green leeks, crème fraîche and parsley and heat through. Spoon on to plates and top with the fish.

Tomato & caraway prawns

This may seem an unusual combination, but it really works. Serve with a green salad and some crusty bread to mop up the juices.

Serves 4
Preparation time: 25 minutes
Cooking time: 20 minutes

2 tablespoons **olive oil**
2 **garlic cloves**, sliced finely
1 teaspoon **caraway seeds**
¼ teaspoon dried **chilli flakes**
1 **green pepper**, de-seeded and finely chopped
400 g can **chopped tomatoes**
a pinch of **caster sugar**
salt and freshly ground **black pepper**
350 g (12 oz) peeled cooked **prawns**, defrosted if frozen
1 tablespoon chopped fresh **coriander**, to garnish

Heat the oil in a large saucepan and fry the garlic until just golden. Add the caraway seeds, chilli flakes and green pepper, and stir well.

Add the tomatoes and sugar and season. Simmer for 20 minutes until the pepper is soft and the sauce thickened.

Add the prawns and reheat for 3 minutes. Serve immediately, sprinkled with the chopped coriander.

Provençal fish casserole

Many traditional Provençal dishes feature generous amounts of garlic. This uses just a couple of cloves, but if you prefer a stronger flavour, add more.

Serves 4
Preparation time:
  40 minutes
Cooking time:
  20–25 minutes

2–3 tablespoons **olive oil**
2 large **onions**, roughly chopped
2 **garlic cloves**, roughly chopped
2 tablespoons coarsely chopped fresh **parsley**, plus extra to garnish
450 g (1 lb) **tomatoes**, skinned and roughly chopped
125 ml (4 fl oz) **dry white wine**
1 teaspoon fresh or ½ teaspoon dried **marjoram**
salt and freshly ground **black pepper**
1 tablespoon **tomato purée**
4 **cod steaks** (approx 675 g/1½ lb total weight), skinned
50 g (1¾ oz) stoned **black olives**

Preheat the oven to 160°C/320°F/Gas Mark 3. Heat the oil in a large flameproof roasting tin and gently fry the onions, garlic and parsley over a low heat for 5–8 minutes.

Add the tomatoes, mix well and then stir in the wine and marjoram. Season and simmer, uncovered, for about 15 minutes. Stir in the tomato purée.

Place the cod steaks in the tin and cover with the sauce. Add the olives. Place the tin in the oven and cook for 20–25 minutes. Serve garnished with fresh parsley.

Variation Any firm-fleshed white fish such as monkfish or haddock can replace the cod in this dish.

Creamy fish pie

There's no fiddly sauce to make for these individual pies, just assemble the base and then top with mash.

Serves 4
Preparation time:
  30 minutes
Cooking time:
  20–25 minutes

550 g (1 lb 3 oz) **fish pie mix**
4 **spring onions**, thinly
  sliced
80 g (3 oz) frozen
  sweetcorn, just defrosted
zest of a small **lemon**
40 g (1½ oz) **Cheddar
  cheese**, grated
300 ml (10 fl oz) **double
  cream**
6 tablespoons **white wine**
  or **milk**
1 **garlic clove**, finely
  chopped (optional)
salt and freshly ground
  black pepper

Topping
800 g (1 lb 11 oz) **potatoes**,
  peeled and chopped
1 **egg**, beaten
3–4 tablespoons **milk**
80 g (3 oz) **Cheddar cheese**,
  grated

Preheat the oven to 200°C/400°F/Gas Mark 6. Combine the fish pie mix with the spring onions, sweetcorn, lemon zest and Cheddar cheese and divide between four 400 ml (14 fl oz) individual pie or ovenproof dishes.

Mix the cream, wine or milk and garlic, if using, together and season. Pour over the fish.

Bring a pan of water to the boil and cook the potatoes for 15 minutes until tender. Drain and mash with half the beaten egg and enough milk to make a smooth creamy mash. Season and mix with two-thirds of the Cheddar cheese.

Spoon the mash over the fish, brush with the remaining egg and sprinkle with the remaining cheese. Put the dishes on a baking tray and bake for 20–25 minutes until the top is golden and the fish base is bubbling and piping hot.

Tip If you are very short of time then cheat and use ready-made chilled mash from the supermarket.

Bean & vegetable hotpot

Easy to make, this colourful dish is good with naan bread, rice or a jacket potato. The flavour is even better if stored in the fridge for a day or two.

Serves 6
Preparation time: 15 minutes
Cooking time: 1½–1¾ hours

1 small **aubergine**, sliced and larger slices halved
1 tablespoon **lemon juice**
2 **garlic cloves**, finely chopped
1 large **onion**, chopped
1 **red pepper**, de-seeded and finely diced
1 **yellow pepper**, de-seeded and finely diced
1 **green pepper**, de-seeded and finely diced
400 g can **kidney beans**, drained and rinsed
2 x 400 g cans **chopped tomatoes with herbs**
2 tablespoons fresh or 2 teaspoons dried **basil**
2 **courgettes**, sliced
225 g (8 oz) frozen **sweetcorn**
freshly ground **black pepper**

Brush the aubergine slices with the lemon juice to prevent browning.

Put the garlic, onion, peppers, kidney beans, tomatoes and basil into a large lidded saucepan. Cover, bring to the boil and simmer for 30 minutes, until the vegetables are beginning to soften.

Add the courgettes and aubergine, bring back to the boil and simmer for a further 45–60 minutes.

Add the sweetcorn, bring back to the boil and simmer for 5 minutes. Season to taste with black pepper.

Tip If you wish, add 4 tablespoons of port with the sweetcorn.

Squash & rocket risotto

Full of fibre, pearl barley makes a change from the more usual rice-based risotto. If you don't like blue cheese, use Parmesan instead.

Serves 4
Preparation time:
  15 minutes
Cooking time:
  65–70 minutes

40 g (1½ oz) unsalted **butter**
1 tablespoon **olive oil**
1 **onion**, thinly sliced
200 g (7 oz) **pearl barley**
1 litre (1¾ pints) **vegetable stock**
salt and freshly ground **black pepper**
450 g (1 lb) **butternut squash**, peeled, de-seeded and diced
50 g (1¾ oz) **blue cheese**, crumbled

To garnish
25 g (1 oz) **rocket**
3 tablespoons **pine nuts**, lightly toasted
crumbled **blue cheese** (optional)

Heat the butter and oil in a large lidded saucepan, add the onion and fry gently for 5 minutes, stirring occasionally until just beginning to colour.

Stir in the pearl barley and stock and season. Bring to the boil, cover and simmer gently for 40 minutes.

Stir in the butternut squash, cover again and cook for a further 25–30 minutes until the squash is tender, stirring from time to time and more frequently towards the end of cooking as the barley absorbs more of the stock.

Stir in the cheese, spoon into large shallow bowls and top with the rocket, pine nuts and a little extra cheese, if using.

Coconut vegetable curry

This is a straightforward vegetable curry. You can make it hotter by adding an extra chilli or more curry paste. Serve with rice or naan bread.

Serves 4
Preparation and
**   cooking time: 1 hour**

1 **onion**, chopped
1 **potato**, peeled and
    chopped
1 small **aubergine**, chopped
1 **carrot**, peeled and
    chopped
1 small **red pepper**,
    de-seeded and chopped
1 small **green pepper**,
    de-seeded and chopped
2 **garlic cloves**, crushed
1 **green** or **red chilli**,
    de-seeded and finely
    chopped
2.5 cm (1 inch) fresh **root**
    ginger, finely chopped
2 tablespoons good quality
    curry paste (medium or
    hot)
75 g (2¾ oz) **creamed**
    coconut, chopped
juice of ½ a **lemon**
2 tablespoons chopped
    fresh **coriander**
salt and freshly ground
    black pepper

Put all the vegetables in a large saucepan with the garlic, chilli and ginger. Cover with about 300–350 ml (10–12 fl oz) of water. Bring to the boil and stir in the curry paste.

Simmer gently until the vegetables are tender, about 20 minutes, adding a little more water if needed.

Add the creamed coconut, stirring gently to mix and then add the lemon juice and coriander. Check the seasoning and serve.

Vegetable korma

Serves 4
Preparation and
cooking time: 1 hour

1 **potato**, peeled and cubed
2 **carrots**, peeled and cubed
10–12 **cauliflower florets**
1 **green pepper**, de-seeded
and cubed
100 g (3½ oz) **peas**
100 g (3½ oz) **green beans**
2 tablespoons **vegetable oil**
1 teaspoon **mustard seeds**
1 **onion**, sliced
3 **garlic cloves**, crushed
2.5 cm (1 inch) fresh **root**
ginger, finely chopped
2 tablespoons **desiccated**
coconut
400 g can **chopped**
tomatoes
400 g (14 oz) **natural yogurt**
1 teaspoon **garam masala**
1 teaspoon **ground**
coriander
1 teaspoon **ground cumin**
¼–½ teaspoon **chilli**
powder
½ teaspoon **turmeric**
50 g (1¾ oz) **ground almonds**
salt and freshly ground
black pepper
chopped fresh **coriander**,
to garnish

Bring a large saucepan of water to the boil and add the potato, carrots and cauliflower. Simmer for 5 minutes. Add the green pepper, peas and beans, bring back up to simmering point and cook for a further 3–4 minutes. Drain the vegetables and set aside.

Heat the oil in the pan and stir in the mustard seeds. When they start to pop, add the onion, garlic and ginger and cook gently for 5–6 minutes to soften the onion. Stir in the desiccated coconut and cook for a further minute and then add the chopped tomatoes.

Meanwhile, mix together the yogurt, spices and ground almonds.

Add the vegetables to the onion and tomato mixture. Lower the heat and carefully stir in the spiced yoghurt. Stir carefully to combine the sauce with the vegetables and simmer gently for a further 8–10 minutes until the vegetables are completely tender. If you prefer a slightly thinner sauce, stir in up to 100 ml (3½ fl oz) of water.

Check the seasoning and serve with a sprinkling of chopped coriander leaves.

Tip If you have a mill to grind the desiccated coconut to a finer texture, it improves the look of the sauce.

Vegetable satay stir-fry

A tasty combination of crunchy stir-fried vegetables in a spicy peanut sauce makes a satisfying vegetarian main course.

Serves 4
Preparation time:
 20 minutes
Cooking time:
 10 minutes

80 g (3 oz) **green beans**, cut
 into 5 cm (2 inch) pieces
115 g (4¼ oz) **broccoli**,
 sliced diagonally
2 tablespoons **vegetable oil**
2 **garlic cloves**, sliced
4 thin slices fresh **root
 ginger**
1 **red chilli**, de-seeded
 and finely sliced
115 g (4¼ oz) **mangetout**
2 **celery sticks**, sliced
 diagonally
50 g (1¾ oz) **courgettes**
 cut into strips
150 ml (5 fl oz) **vegetable
 stock**
4 tablespoons smooth
 peanut butter
50 g (1¾ oz) roasted salted
 peanuts
salt and freshly ground
 black pepper

Bring a large shallow pan of water to the boil, add the beans and broccoli and blanch for 30 seconds. Drain and refresh in cold water, drain again.

Heat the oil in the pan, add the garlic, ginger and chilli and stir fry to release the flavours.

Reduce the heat, add the mangetout to the pan and stir fry for 1 minute. Add the celery, courgettes, broccoli and beans to the pan and stir fry for another minute until the vegetables are cooked but still crisp and bright green.

Stir in the vegetable stock and peanut butter and heat through until bubbling. Add the peanuts, season and simmer for 2 minutes. Serve immediately.

Spicy Moroccan vegetables

Seven vegetables are used in this dish, as seven is considered a lucky number in Morocco. Choose from those listed and serve with couscous.

Serves 6
Preparation and cooking time:
1½ hours

1 tablespoon **olive oil**
1 **onion**, chopped
400 g can **chopped tomatoes**
1 vegetable **stock cube**
1 **garlic clove**, crushed
½ teaspoon dried **chilli flakes**
1 teaspoon **ground cumin**
salt and freshly ground **black pepper**
2 tablespoons chopped fresh **parsley**

Vegetables
225 g (8 oz) **new potatoes**
2 **carrots**
1 small **white cabbage**
1 **turnip**
1 **parsnip**
175 g (6 oz) **broad beans**
4 **celery sticks**
1 small **aubergine**
1 small **sweet potato**
½ **butternut squash**

Choose six vegetables from those listed (the onion is the seventh) and prepare them, peeling, de-seeding and cutting into chunks where necessary.

Heat the oil in a large saucepan and fry the onion until golden. Add the tomatoes, stock cube, garlic, chilli flakes and cumin. Season, add 300 ml (10 fl oz) of water, and bring to the boil.

Add whichever six vegetables you are using in rotation, starting with the new potatoes, carrots or cabbage. Cover and simmer for 10 minutes.

Next add the turnip, parsnip, broad beans or celery and cook for a further 10 minutes. Lastly add the aubergine, sweet potato or squash and cook for another 10 minutes.

Serve sprinkled with the parsley.

Tip The secret is to cook whichever vegetables you select in the right order, so follow the sequence of cooking given here.

Lentil & vegetable curry

Serve this really simple curry as a main course for four with garlic and coriander naan bread or as an accompanying vegetable dish for eight.

Serves 4
Preparation time:
  20 minutes
Cooking time: 1 hour

2 tablespoons **vegetable oil**
1 **onion**, finely chopped
2 **garlic cloves**, crushed
2 tablespoons **curry powder**
1 teaspoon **turmeric**
6 **cardamom pods**, crushed
½ teaspoon **ground
  cinnamon**
2 **bay leaves**
115 g (4¼ oz) **red lentils**,
  rinsed well
1 **aubergine**, cubed
2 **carrots**, peeled and sliced
1 **cauliflower**, divided into
  small florets
175 g (6 oz) **okra**, each cut
  into 3
3 tablespoons chopped
  fresh **coriander**

To garnish
4 tablespoons **natural
  yogurt**
mango chutney

Heat the oil in a large lidded saucepan and fry the onion and garlic until soft. Add the spices and bay leaves and cook for 1 minute. Add the lentils, aubergine, carrots and cauliflower and cook for 5 minutes.

Pour in 850 ml (1½ pints) of water and bring to the boil. Reduce to a gentle simmer, cover and cook gently for 1 hour.

Add the okra and coriander and cook for 5 minutes. Serve garnished with the yogurt swirled with a little mango chutney.

Mushrooms in red wine

Serve poured over plain Quorn fillets, stir fried tofu or steamed individual cauliflowers. It is also excellent over beef or turkey steaks.

Serves 3
Preparation time:
  10 minutes
Cooking time:
  40 minutes

25 g (1 oz) unsalted **butter**
1 **red onion**, finely chopped
110 g (4 oz) **button mushrooms**, sliced
55 g (2 oz) **chestnut mushrooms**, sliced
55 g (2 oz) **oyster mushrooms**, sliced
4 tablespoons **brandy**
200 ml (7 fl oz) **red wine**
2 teaspoons **plain flour** or **cornflour**
150 ml (5 fl oz) hot **vegetable stock**
freshly ground **black pepper**

Heat the butter in a lidded heavy-based pan, add the onion, cover and cook over a gentle heat until tender, this should take about 20 minutes. Remove with a slotted spoon and set aside.

Add the mushrooms to the pan and stir fry for 2 minutes over a medium heat. Add the brandy, bring to the boil and simmer without a lid for 1–2 minutes, until the liquid is reduced by half. Pour in the red wine, return the onion to the pan and simmer for 5 minutes.

Mix the flour or cornflour with a little cold water and blend to a smooth paste. Stir the stock into the paste. Pour the blended stock into the pan and bring to the boil, stirring all the time.

Simmer gently for about 15 minutes, until the sauce has a syrupy consistency. Season to taste with black pepper.

Beetroot chilli

Preparing beetroot can be a messy business, so don a pair of rubber gloves before you begin to avoid pink hands. Serve with soft tortillas or rice.

Serves 4
Preparation time:
  45 minutes
Cooking time:
  45 minutes

2 tablespoons **sunflower oil**
1 **onion**, chopped
200 g (7 oz) **button mushrooms**, halved
2 **garlic cloves**, finely chopped
1 teaspoon dried **chilli flakes**
1 teaspoon **ground cumin**
½ teaspoon **ground cinnamon**
500 g (1 lb 2 oz) **beetroot**, peeled and cut into 2 cm (¾ inch) dice
400 g can **kidney beans**, drained and rinsed
400 g can **chopped tomatoes**
1 tablespoon **light muscovado sugar**
450 ml (16 fl oz) **vegetable stock**
salt and freshly ground **black pepper**

Heat the oil in a large lidded saucepan, add the onion and fry for 5 minutes, stirring from time to time until softened. Add the mushrooms and garlic and fry for 5 minutes.

Add the chilli flakes, cumin, cinnamon, beetroot, kidney beans, tomatoes, sugar and stock and season well. Bring to the boil, stirring.

Cover and simmer gently for 45 minutes, stirring from time to time and topping up with a little extra stock if needed until the beetroot is tender. Serve.

Tip Serve garnished with soured cream and a tomato salsa made from 2 diced tomatoes, 3 finely chopped spring onions and a small bunch of chopped fresh coriander leaves.

Chestnut gratin

Serves 4
Preparation and cooking time:
65–70 minutes

2 tablespoons **olive oil**
1 **red onion**, chopped
1 **aubergine**, cut into 2 cm
   (¾ inch) cubes
2 **leeks**, thickly sliced
2 **celery sticks**, thickly
   sliced
½ teaspoon **ground ginger**
½ teaspoon freshly grated
   nutmeg
a large pinch of **ground**
   cloves
1 tablespoon **plain flour**
250 ml (8 fl oz) **vegetable**
   stock
150 ml (5 fl oz) **red wine**
1 tablespoon **tomato purée**
salt and freshly ground
   black pepper
240 g can peeled cooked
   chestnuts

Topping
50 g (1¾ oz) **crusty bread**,
   torn into small pieces
2 fresh **rosemary sprigs**,
   leaves roughly chopped
25 g (1 oz) fresh **Parmesan**
   cheese, grated
1 tablespoon **olive oil**

Preheat the oven to 190°C/375°F/Gas Mark 5. Heat the oil in a shallow, lidded, flameproof and ovenproof casserole dish, add the onion and aubergine and fry for 5 minutes, stirring until just beginning to soften and brown. Add the leeks, celery and spices and cook for 1 minute.

Sprinkle the flour over the top and stir the vegetables to mix. Pour over the stock and red wine and then mix in the tomato purée. Season. Add the chestnuts, cover and simmer gently for 10 minutes.

Mix the bread for the topping with the rosemary and Parmesan. Remove the lid from the casserole dish, sprinkle the crumbs over the top and drizzle with the oil. Bake, uncovered, for 20–25 minutes until golden.

Squash & lentil casserole

Ginger gives a warm flavour to this casserole, making it ideal for cold winter days. Serve with steamed rice if you wish.

Serves 4
Preparation time:
  15 minutes
Cooking time:
  40-45 minutes

1 tablespoon **vegetable oil**
1 **onion**, sliced
1 **garlic clove**, crushed
2.5 cm (1 inch) fresh **root ginger**, grated
1 **butternut squash**, peeled, de-seeded and chopped
1 **yellow pepper**, de-seeded and cubed
½ teaspoon **ground cumin**
1 teaspoon **ground coriander**
150 ml (5 fl oz) **vegetable stock**
400 g can **chopped tomatoes**
400 g can **lentils**, drained and rinsed
400 g can **cannellini beans**, drained and rinsed
100 g (3½ oz) **baby spinach leaves**, washed
1 tablespoon chopped fresh **coriander**
freshly ground **black pepper**

Heat the oil in a large flameproof casserole dish or a saucepan and gently cook the onion for 4–5 minutes until beginning to soften. Add the garlic and ginger and cook for a further 2–3 minutes.

Stir in the butternut squash, pepper, cumin and coriander and sauté gently for 5 minutes. Add the stock and tomatoes and bring up to the boil. Reduce the heat, cover the pan and simmer for 20–25 minutes until the butternut squash is tender.

Add the lentils and beans, stir through and continue to cook for a further 5 minutes until the beans are thoroughly warmed through. Add the spinach and coriander and stir through for 3 minutes until the spinach is wilted. Season to taste with black pepper and serve immediately.

Asparagus quiche

Fresh asparagus and Gruyère cheese combine well to make a subtle filling for this delicious quiche.

Serves 4
Preparation time:
  20 minutes +
  30 minutes chilling
Cooking time:
  50–55 minutes

Wholemeal pastry
115 g (4¼ oz) **wholemeal flour**
1 teaspoon **baking powder**
25 g (1 oz) **butter** or **block margarine**, cubed
25 g (1 oz) **white vegetable fat**, cubed

Filling
80 g (3 oz) **asparagus tips**
80 g (3 oz) **Gruyère cheese**, grated
2 large **eggs**, plus 1 **egg yolk**
250 ml (9 fl oz) **semi-skimmed milk**
½ teaspoon **Dijon mustard**
freshly ground **black pepper**

Mix the flour and baking powder together in a bowl and rub in the butter or margarine and vegetable fat until the mixture resembles fine breadcrumbs. Sprinkle over 2 tablespoons of cold water and bring it together to form a ball of dough.

Roll out the pastry thinly on a lightly floured surface, and use it to line a deep 20 cm (8 inch) flan tin. Prick the base with a fork and chill for at least 30 minutes. Preheat the oven to 200°C/400°F/Gas Mark 6 and place a baking tray on the middle shelf.

Line the pastry case with a sheet of foil, greaseproof paper or non-stick baking parchment and fill with baking beans. Bake blind for 15 minutes. Remove the lining and beans and return to the oven for a further 5 minutes, until lightly golden.

Meanwhile, bring a saucepan of water to the boil and blanch the asparagus tips for 2 minutes. Drain and plunge them into cold water to stop them from cooking.

Remove the pastry case from the oven and reduce the temperature to 190°C/375°F/ Gas Mark 5.

Scatter the grated cheese over the base of the pastry case. Whisk together the eggs, egg yolk, milk and mustard and season with black pepper. Pour the mixture over the cheese. Drain the asparagus and arrange the tips on top.

Return the quiche to the oven and bake for 30–35 minutes, until puffy and golden. Serve warm or cold.

Lamb shish kebabs

A traditional Middle Eastern dish, 'shish' kebab is a popular takeaway of spit-roasted lamb, sliced and served in pitta bread.

Serves 4
Preparation time:
   20 minutes +
   overnight marinating
Cooking time:
   20 minutes

450 g (1 lb) **lamb neck** or
   shoulder fillet, trimmed
   of all visible fat
2 fresh **rosemary sprigs**,
   bruised
1 **garlic clove**, thinly sliced
1 tablespoon **olive oil**
1 tablespoon **lemon juice**
freshly ground **black pepper**

To serve
4 **plain** or **wholemeal pitta**
   breads
½ **Cos** or **Romaine lettuce**,
   shredded
2 ripe **tomatoes**, diced
1 small **red onion**, thinly
   sliced
houmous or **tzatziki**

Place the lamb fillets in a bowl with the rosemary and garlic. Pour over the oil and lemon juice. Season with pepper and stir thoroughly to coat the meat. Cover and leave to marinate overnight if possible. Stir a couple of times.

Preheat the oven to 240°C/475°F/Gas Mark 9. Place a roasting tin in the oven on the highest shelf.

Scrape the rosemary leaves and garlic off the lamb. Place the fillets in the preheated roasting tin, taking care as the meat may spit. Cook for 20 minutes. Remove from the oven and allow the lamb to rest for 10 minutes.

Lightly toast or warm the pitta breads. Split them horizontally and fill with the lettuce, tomatoes and onion. Thinly slice the lamb and divide it between the pockets. Add some houmous or tzatziki to each pocket and serve at once.

Artichoke & salami pizza

Serves 3
Preparation and cooking time:
   1 hour

225 g (8 oz) **strong white bread flour**
1 teaspoon **easy-blend dried yeast**
½ teaspoon **coarse sea salt**
1 tablespoon **olive oil**

Topping
2 teaspoons **extra virgin olive oil**
150 ml (5 fl oz) **passata**
1 **garlic clove**, chopped finely
15 g (½ oz) fresh **basil leaves**, a few reserved to garnish and the rest torn
½ × 390 g can **artichoke hearts**, drained and halved
115 g (4¼ oz) **button mushrooms**, sliced
25 g (1 oz) **Italian salami with peppercorns**, slices halved
125 g (4½ oz) **buffalo mozzarella**, sliced thinly
½ small **red onion**, sliced thinly
12 **black olives**
15 g (½ oz) **Parmesan cheese** shavings, to garnish

Combine the flour, yeast and salt in a bowl. Make a well in the centre and pour in the oil and 150 ml (5 fl oz) of warm water. Mix to combine and then tip out on to a work surface and knead for 10 minutes until the dough is smooth. Place in an oiled polythene bag, in a warm place, for about 15 minutes.

Preheat the oven to 220°C/425°F/Gas Mark 7. Grease a baking tray.

Either roll out the dough on a lightly floured work surface or shape with your hands into a 30 cm (12 inch) round. Place on the baking tray and brush lightly with 1 teaspoon of the oil.

Smooth the passata evenly over the surface and scatter with the garlic and basil. Top with the remaining ingredients.

Cover loosely with an oiled polythene bag and leave in a warm place for 15 minutes to enable the dough to puff up slightly.

Remove the bag and drizzle the remaining teaspoon of oil over the pizza. Bake in the centre of the oven for 15–20 minutes. Check after 15 minutes and dab off any liquid that has come out of the mushrooms with a little kitchen towel. Return to the oven for a further 5 minutes if you like a crisp pizza.

Serve garnished with the Parmesan shavings and reserved basil sprigs.

Cornish pasties

Pasties are a classic example of how just a few good-quality ingredients can achieve a delicious result. They are best eaten warm.

Makes 6
Preparation time:
   25 minutes
Cooking time:
   40 minutes

Pastry
80 g (3 oz) **butter** or
   block margarine, cubed
80 g (3 oz) **white vegetable**
   fat, cubed
350 g (12 oz) **plain flour**
1 **egg**, beaten, to glaze

Filling
350 g (12 oz) **steak mince**
175 g (6 oz) **potato**, peeled,
   very thinly sliced and
   roughly chopped
175 g (6 oz) **turnip**, peeled,
   very thinly sliced and
   roughly chopped
1 **onion**, finely chopped
¼ teaspoon **dried mixed**
   herbs
a good pinch of **cayenne**
   pepper
sea salt and freshly ground
   black pepper

Preheat the oven to 220°C/425°F/Gas Mark 7. Lightly grease a baking tray.

For the pastry, rub the butter or margarine and vegetable fat into the flour until the mixture resembles fine breadcrumbs. Sprinkle over 6 tablespoons of cold water and bring it all together to form a ball of dough. Wrap in cling film and chill in the fridge while you make the filling.

In a bowl, combine the mince, potato, turnip and onion. Add the herbs and cayenne pepper and season. Stir in 2 tablespoons of cold water to moisten.

Divide the pastry into six. On a lightly floured surface, roll out each piece into a 20 cm (8 inch) circle. Do not worry if the edges are a little uneven, it just adds to the rugged effect.

Dampen the edges with a little milk. Place a portion of the meat filling on half of each circle, fold over the pastry to cover and press the edges together to seal. Roll the pasties over so the edges are on the top and crimp with your fingers to form the traditional wavy pattern. Place on the baking tray, brush with the beaten egg and make two slits near the top of each side to allow steam to escape.

Bake in the middle of the oven for 10 minutes before reducing the heat to 180°C/350°F/Gas Mark 4 for a further 30 minutes, or until the pasties are golden and the filling cooked.

Lamb & apple burger

Cook these on the barbecue and serve with salad leaves and tomato slices. Or grill them and serve with potato wedges and a spicy tomato relish.

Makes 6–8
Preparation and cooking time:
25 minutes

450 g (1 lb) lean **lamb mince**
1 small **onion**, grated
1 small **eating apple**,
    peeled, cored and grated
1 teaspoon **ground cumin**
1 **chilli**, de-seeded and
    finely chopped
1 **egg**, beaten
50 g (1¾ oz) fresh
    wholemeal breadcrumbs
salt and freshly ground
    black pepper
1 tablespoon **sunflower oil**

To serve
1 **ciabatta bread**, sliced
1 **Little Gem lettuce**, torn
4 **tomatoes**, sliced
tomato chutney

Place the mince in a mixing bowl and add the onion, apple, cumin, chilli, egg, breadcrumbs and seasoning. Mix thoroughly. Shape the mixture into 6–8 even-sized burgers.

Brush both sides of the burgers with the oil and cook on a preheated grill or barbecue for 5–7 minutes, on each side, until cooked right through.

Serve between slices of the ciabatta bread, together with the lettuce, tomatoes and tomato chutney.

Tagliatelle bolognese

A classic Italian dish that is popular worldwide. This version includes white wine to produce a light sauce that is really delicious.

Serves 4
Preparation time:
  25 minutes
Cooking time:
  30–40 minutes

15 g (½ oz) **butter**
50 g (1¾ oz) lean **back bacon**, chopped
2 **garlic cloves**, finely chopped
1 large **onion**, finely chopped
2 **carrots**, peeled and diced
2 **celery sticks**, chopped
500 g (1 lb 2 oz) lean **beef mince**
400g can **chopped tomatoes**
3 tablespoons **tomato purée**
1 teaspoon **dried oregano**
150 ml (5 fl oz) **dry white wine**
150 ml (5 fl oz) **beef stock**
salt and freshly ground **black pepper**
225 g (8 oz) **tagliatelle**
grated **Parmesan cheese**, to serve

Melt the butter in a deep frying pan, add the bacon and fry for 2–3 minutes. Add the garlic, onion, carrots and celery and fry for 5 minutes until lightly browned. Add the mince and brown lightly.

Stir in the tomatoes, tomato purée, oregano, wine and stock, season and bring to the boil. Lower the heat and simmer for 30–40 minutes until the sauce is reduced and thick.

Meanwhile, bring a saucepan of water to the boil and cook the tagliatelle according to the packet instructions until just al dente.

Drain the tagliatelle and toss with the meat sauce. Sprinkle with grated Parmesan cheese to serve.

Spaghetti carbonara

This is a dream to make; you can rustle it up in next to no time. It also has the added bonus of being healthier than ready-made versions.

Serves 4
Preparation time:
  10 minutes
Cooking time:
  10 minutes

350 g (12 oz) **spaghetti**
1 tablespoon **olive oil**
175 g (6 oz) lean **back bacon**, snipped into pieces
3 **eggs**, lightly beaten
4 tablespoons grated **Parmesan cheese**
4 tablespoons **fromage frais**
freshly ground **black pepper**

To serve
1 tablespoon chopped fresh **parsley**
shaved **Parmesan cheese**

Bring a large saucepan of water to the boil and cook the spaghetti according to the packet instructions until just al dente.

Meanwhile, heat the oil in a frying pan. Add the bacon and fry over a high heat for about 5 minutes, until crisp and golden.

Beat together the eggs, Parmesan and fromage frais. Season with pepper to taste. Drain the pasta well and return it to the saucepan, away from direct heat.

Discard all but 1 tablespoon of fat from the bacon. Add this, plus the bacon, to the spaghetti, making sure that you scrape in any tasty, crunchy bits stuck to the bottom of the frying pan.

Pour in the egg mixture and mix everything together. Keep stirring until the spaghetti is thoroughly coated and the sauce is creamy and smooth. Serve at once, sprinkled with the parsley, Parmesan and a grinding of black pepper.

Tip Don't be tempted to return the pan to the hob after you have added the sauce – the eggs will scramble; just allow the heat of the pasta to cook the sauce through.

Mushroom tagliatelle

Wild mushrooms have a lot more flavour than regular mushrooms, but if you can't find them, any other mushrooms will do.

Serves 4
Preparation time:
  10 minutes
Cooking time:
  15 minutes

350 g (12 oz) **tagliatelle**
4 tablespoons **olive oil**
2 fat **garlic cloves**, thinly
  sliced
175 g (6 oz) **wild
  mushrooms**, roughly
  chopped
salt and freshly ground
  black pepper
2 tablespoons chopped
  fresh **parsley**

Bring a large saucepan of water to the boil and cook the tagliatelle according to the packet instructions until just al dente

Meanwhile, heat the oil in a small saucepan and fry the garlic slices until just beginning to brown.

Add the mushrooms to the garlic and cook for 4–5 minutes until the mushrooms soften and release their juices. Season.

Drain the pasta, return to the saucepan and pour over the mushroom mixture. Stir to mix and sprinkle in the parsley. Serve immediately.

Macaroni cheese

A classic family favourite, this ever-popular dish is always a hit with children and adults alike. Serve simply with a green salad.

Serves 3–4
Preparation time:
20 minutes
Cooking time:
15 minutes

225 g (8 oz) quick-cook
  macaroni

Cheese sauce
40 g (1½ oz) **butter**
40 g (1½ oz) **plain flour**
600 ml (20 fl oz)
  semi-skimmed milk
salt, cayenne pepper and
  mustard powder, to taste
175 g (6 oz) **Cheddar**
  cheese, grated
50 g (1¾ oz) **wholemeal**
  breadcrumbs

Bring a large saucepan of water to the boil and cook the macaroni according to the packet instructions until just al dente. Drain well.

For the cheese sauce, melt the butter in a saucepan. Add the flour and cook for 1 minute, stirring continuously with a wooden spoon. Remove the pan from the heat and gradually stir in the milk.

Return the pan to the heat and bring to the boil, stirring continuously to avoid lumps. Cook the sauce for 1 minute, still stirring continuously. Remove from the heat and add salt, cayenne pepper and mustard powder to taste. Add half the cheese and stir until it has melted. Preheat the grill to medium-high.

Mix the macaroni and cheese sauce together and place in a 1.7 litre (3 pint) pie dish. Mix together the remaining cheese and the breadcrumbs and sprinkle evenly over the top.

Toast under the grill until golden brown and serve immediately.

Ham & tomato pasta bake

This is ideal for using up any ham left over at Christmas time. Serve with a selection of lightly cooked green vegetables or a crisp green salad.

Serves 4
Preparation time:
  20 minutes
Cooking time:
  25–30 minutes

175 g (6 oz) **fusilli**
1 tablespoon **vegetable oil**
1 **onion**, chopped
2 **garlic cloves**, chopped
200 g (7 oz) **cooked ham**, cubed
400 g can **chopped tomatoes**
1 teaspoon **dried basil**
300 ml (10 fl oz) **semi-skimmed milk**
2 **eggs**
1 tablespoon **tomato purée**
freshly ground **black pepper**
75 g (2¾ oz) **mature Cheddar cheese**, grated

Preheat the oven to 180°C/350°F/Gas Mark 4.

Bring a large saucepan of water to the boil and cook the fusilli according to the packet instructions until just al dente. Drain thoroughly.

Meanwhile, heat the oil in a large frying pan and fry the onion and garlic for 5 minutes to soften. Add the ham, tomatoes and basil and simmer for 8–10 minutes.

Stir the cooked pasta gently into the ham and tomato mixture and stir gently to combine. Turn the mixture into a shallow ovenproof dish.

Whisk together the milk, eggs and tomato purée and season with black pepper. Pour the egg mixture over the pasta and sprinkle the grated Cheddar cheese over the top.

Bake for 25–30 minutes until the mixture is set and the top is golden brown. Serve immediately.

Beef olives

A time-honoured dish of slices of beef rolled around a simple vegetable stuffing. Serve with baby new potatoes and mixed roasted vegetables.

Serves 4
Preparation time:
  20 minutes
Cooking time:
  1½–2 hours

450 g (1 lb) **topside of beef**
salt and freshly ground
  black pepper
2 teaspoons **cornflour**
2 small **carrots**, peeled
  and finely diced
1 small **onion**, finely diced
1 teaspoon **dried mixed**
  herbs
1 tablespoon **tomato purée**
1 tablespoon
  Worcestershire sauce
150 ml (5 fl oz) **beef stock**
150 ml (5 fl oz) **red wine**
4 rashers **unsmoked streaky**
  bacon
1 tablespoon finely chopped
  fresh **parsley**, to garnish
  (optional)

Preheat the oven to 180°C/350°F/Gas Mark 4. Carve the topside into four thick slices. Place each slice between sheets of greaseproof paper and flatten them by bashing with a rolling pin or meat hammer. Season.

Blend the cornflour with a little cold water to make a paste. In a bowl, mix together the carrots, onion, herbs, tomato purée, Worcestershire sauce, blended cornflour and 4 tablespoons of the stock.

Divide the stuffing mixture between the flattened slices and roll up each into a neat parcel. Wrap each parcel with a rasher of bacon and tie securely with string.

Place the parcels in a shallow roasting tin or ovenproof baking dish and pour in the remaining stock and the red wine. Cover the dish tightly with foil and cook for 1½–2 hours or until the meat is really tender.

To serve, remove the string from each parcel and garnish with the parsley, if using. These aer delicious served with ratatouille.

Tip Ask your butcher to cut four slices of topside for you, rather than buying one big piece.

Moussaka

Make this ahead and then cook for when your friends arrive; all it needs is a crisp salad of mixed leaves to accompany.

Serves 4
Preparation and cooking time: 2 hours

450 g (1 lb) **aubergines**
sea salt
450 g (1 lb) lean **lamb mince**
1 large **onion**, finely chopped
1 tablespoon **plain flour**
400 g can **chopped tomatoes**
1 fat **garlic clove**, crushed
2 teaspoons **tomato purée**
1 tablespoon chopped fresh **parsley**
1 teaspoon **ground cinnamon**
½ teaspoon **dried oregano**
1 **bay leaf**
freshly ground **black pepper**
2–3 tablespoons **olive oil**
450 g (1 lb) **cooked waxy potatoes**, sliced

Topping
300 g (10½ oz) **Greek yogurt**
2 **eggs**, beaten
50 g (1¾ oz) **Parmesan cheese**, finely grated
a little freshly grated **nutmeg**

Remove the stalks from the aubergines and cut into 1 cm (½ inch) slices. Layer in a colander, sprinkling a little salt between each layer. Weigh down and leave for 30 minutes to extract any bitter juices.

Meanwhile, brown the mince and onion in a non-stick lidded saucepan over a high heat, breaking up any lumps. Reduce the heat, stir in the flour and cook for 1 minute. Add the tomatoes, garlic, tomato purée, parsley, cinnamon, oregano and bay leaf. Season, bring to the boil, cover the pan, reduce the heat and simmer for 30 minutes, stirring occasionally. Preheat the grill to high.

Rinse the salt from the aubergines and pat them dry with a tea towel. Arrange in a single layer on the grill pan and brush with half the olive oil. Grill for about 5 minutes, or until golden. Turn, brush with the remaining oil and grill again until golden.

Preheat the oven to 180°C/350°F/Gas Mark 4 and lightly grease a 2.3 litre (4 pint) ovenproof dish.

Remove the bay leaf from the mince and adjust the seasoning if necessary. Arrange half the aubergine slices over the base of the dish, and half the potato slices on top of them. Pour the lamb sauce over the top. Finish with the remaining aubergine and potato slices.

In a bowl, whisk together the yogurt, eggs and Parmesan. Season and pour over the potato, covering it completely. Sprinkle a little grated nutmeg over the top and bake for about 40 minutes, until puffy and golden.

Turkey & leek pie

Instead of brushing the filo pastry with melted butter, use it as it is. The pastry will still bake to an attractive golden colour.

Serves 6
Preparation time:
40 minutes
Cooking time:
20–30 minutes

2 tablespoons **vegetable oil**
750 g (1 lb 10 oz) skinless,
    boneless **turkey breast**,
    cubed
2 **leeks**, sliced
2 **celery sticks**, sliced
1 **onion**, sliced
2 small **carrots**, peeled
    and sliced
2 tablespoons **plain flour**
150 ml (5 fl oz) **dry cider**
300 ml (10 fl oz) **chicken
    stock**
1 tablespoon **Dijon mustard**
2 tablespoons **crème
    fraîche**
freshly ground **black pepper**
6 sheets **filo pastry**
1 teaspoon **sesame seeds**

Preheat the oven to 200°C/400°F/Gas Mark 6.

Heat 1 tablespoon of the oil in a large lidded saucepan and fry the turkey in batches until golden brown. Set aside. Add the vegetables to the pan and gently sauté for 4–5 minutes. Sprinkle over the flour and cook for 1 minute.

Gradually stir in the cider and stock, followed by the mustard, and bring up to the boil, stirring to allow the sauce to thicken. Return the turkey to the pan. Reduce the heat, cover the pan and simmer gently for 15–20 minutes until the vegetables are tender. Stir in the crème fraîche and season with black pepper. Transfer the mixture to a shallow ovenproof dish.

Take one sheet of filo pastry at a time, spread it out on a clean work surface and lightly brush with the remaining oil. Crumple each sheet slightly and arrange on top of the turkey mixture to cover it completely. Sprinkle over the sesame seeds.

Bake the pie for 20–30 minutes until the pastry is cooked through and the filling is piping hot. Cover the top with foil if the pastry appears to be browning too quickly. Serve immediately.

Steak, kidney & whisky pie

A traditional comfort food, but with a modern twist – steak, kidney and onions flavoured with whisky and topped with puff pastry.

Serves 4
Preparation time:
2 hours 30 minutes
Cooking time:
30–40 minutes

2 tablespoons **plain flour**
salt and freshly ground
    black pepper
675 g (1 lb 8 oz) **braising**
    steak, diced
225 g (8 oz) **lamb's kidneys**,
    chopped
2 tablespoons **vegetable oil**
1 large **onion**, thinly sliced
4 tablespoons **whisky**
425 ml (15 fl oz) **beef stock**
350 g (12 oz) ready-made
    puff pastry
beaten **egg**, to glaze

Mix together the flour and seasoning on a plate. Coat the steak and kidneys evenly in the seasoned flour.

Heat the oil in a large lidded saucepan and fry the meat for 5–6 minutes until browned all over. Transfer to a plate.

Add the onion to the pan and fry until soft. Stir in the whisky and simmer until all the liquid has evaporated.

Return the meat and juices to the pan and gradually stir in the stock. Season. Cover and simmer gently for 2 hours or until the beef is tender. Leave to cool. Preheat the oven to 200°C/400°F/Gas Mark 6.

Spoon the cooled mixture into a 1 litre (1¾ pint) pie dish. Roll out the pastry 2.5 cm (1 inch) wider than the dish. Cut out a wide strip of pastry to fit the edge of the dish and stick it to the rim with water. Place the pastry lid on the dish and trim if necessary. Crimp the edges. Cut out leaf shapes from any remaining pastry and stick in place with water. Brush with beaten egg and make a slit in the top.

Bake for 30–40 minutes until the pastry is risen and golden.

Shepherd's pie

Traditionally, shepherd's pie is made from lamb and cottage pie from beef. Adding 'hidden' vegetables is an easy way of boosting your 5-a-day.

Serves 4
Preparation and cooking time: 1 hour 30 minutes

450 g (1 lb) **minced lamb**
1 large **onion**, chopped
1 tablespoon **plain flour**
300 ml (10 fl oz) good **lamb stock**
115 g (4 oz) **button mushrooms**, finely sliced
1 tablespoon **Worcestershire sauce**
1 tablespoon **tomato purée**
2 tablespoons chopped fresh **parsley**
1 **bay leaf**
freshly ground **black pepper**

Potato & leek topping
700 g (1 lb 9 oz) **potatoes**, peeled and quartered
25 g (1 oz) **butter**
2 **leeks**, very finely sliced
3 tablespoons **milk**
80 g (3 oz) **Cheddar cheese**, grated

Brown the mince and onion in a large, lidded, non-stick pan over a high heat, breaking up any lumps of meat. Reduce the heat and stir in the flour. Cook through for 1 minute.

Gradually blend in the stock. Add the mushrooms, Worcestershire sauce, tomato purée, parsley and bay leaf and season to taste with pepper. Bring to the boil, cover, reduce the heat and simmer for 30 minutes, until the lamb is cooked. Stir occasionally.

Meanwhile, bring a saucepan of water to the boil, add the potatoes, cover and simmer for 15–20 minutes, or until cooked.

While the potatoes are cooking, melt the butter in a frying pan and sauté the leeks over a low heat for 10 minutes until softened, but not brown.

Preheat the oven to 200°C/400°F/Gas Mark 6. Grease a 2 litre (3½ pint) ovenproof dish.

Drain the potatoes and return to the heat to dry off any excess moisture. Mash until lump free. Beat in the leeks, milk and 50 g (1¾ oz) of the cheese. Adjust the seasoning to taste.

Remove the bay leaf from the mince. Add a little extra stock if the mixture seems dry and then pour into the prepared dish. Spoon the potato over the top and roughly smooth the surface. Sprinkle with the remaining grated cheese and bake for 30 minutes, until the top is crisp and golden. Alternatively brown under a hot grill, whichever is more convenient.

Tips If making in advance and cooking the pie straight from the fridge, it will take about 45 minutes to heat through thoroughly.

Try making this in four individual pie dishes for perfect little servings.

Tomato crusted salmon

Use sunblush or semi-cuit tomatoes for this recipe in preference to sun-dried tomatoes, because they are brighter in colour and more moist.

Serves 4
Preparation time:
  20 minutes
Cooking time:
  15–20 minutes

4 × 150–175 g (5½–6 oz)
  skinless **salmon fillets**
75 g (2¾ oz) fresh **white
  breadcrumbs**
finely grated zest of ½ a
  lemon
25 g (1 oz) stoned **black
  olives**, finely chopped
25 g (1 oz) **sunblush
  tomatoes**, finely chopped
1 tablespoon finely chopped
  fresh **flat leaf parsley**
2 tablespoons **olive oil**

Roasted tomatoes
1 packet **cherry tomatoes**
  on the vine
1 tablespoon **olive oil**
freshly ground **black pepper**

Preheat the oven to 200ºC/400°F/Gas Mark 6. Line a baking tray with non-stick baking parchment and place the salmon fillets on it.

In a small bowl, mix together the breadcrumbs, lemon zest, olives, sunblush tomatoes and parsley. Add the olive oil and stir well to moisten the breadcrumbs and combine the ingredients.

Spoon the breadcrumb mixture evenly over the salmon pieces and press it down lightly to form a crust. Bake in the oven for 15–20 minutes until the salmon is cooked and the breadcrumbs are lightly golden and crusty.

Meanwhile, place the cherry tomatoes, still on their stalks, in a small roasting tin. Drizzle over the olive oil and add a grinding of black pepper. Bake in the oven for 10–15 minutes along with the fish until just tender and softened.

To serve, place a salmon portion on a warmed plate and top each one with a few of the tomatoes still on their vine.

Tomato & spinach lasagne

Tomato, spinach and ricotta are classic flavourings for pasta. Any left over can be frozen and used another time. Serve with a salad.

Serves 4–6
Preparation and cooking time: 70–75 minutes

8 **lasagne sheets**
25 g (1 oz) **Cheddar cheese**, grated
1 tablespoon grated **Parmesan cheese**
torn fresh **basil**, to garnish

Tomato sauce
1 tablespoon **olive oil**
1 **onion**, finely chopped
2 **garlic cloves**, crushed
2 × 400 g cans **chopped tomatoes**
1 tablespoon **tomato purée**
½ teaspoon **dried basil**
½ teaspoon **caster sugar**
150 ml (5 fl oz) **vegetable stock**

Spinach layer
450 g (1 lb) **frozen spinach**, defrosted
250 g (9 oz) **ricotta cheese**
½ teaspoon **ground nutmeg**
freshly ground **black pepper**

Preheat the oven to 190ºC/375°F/Gas Mark 5.

To make the tomato sauce, heat the olive oil in a large lidded saucepan and gently cook the onion and garlic until softened. Add the tomatoes, tomato purée, basil, sugar and stock. Bring up to the boil, cover and then reduce the heat and simmer for 20–25 minutes until the sauce has slightly thickened.

Meanwhile, place the spinach in a sieve and, using the back of a wooden spoon, press against it to remove as much of the excess water as possible. Turn the spinach into a bowl and mix in the ricotta, nutmeg and a good grinding of black pepper.

Pour half the tomato sauce over the base of a shallow 20 × 28 cm (8 × 11 inch) ovenproof dish. Layer four lasagne sheets over the sauce. Spread over the spinach and ricotta mixture, and then layer with the last four lasagne sheets. Cover with the remaining tomato sauce. Sprinkle over the Cheddar cheese and grated Parmesan.

Bake for 25–30 minutes until the cheese on top is melted and lightly browned and the lasagne is heated through. Serve immediately, garnished with the torn basil.

Carrot & chestnut filo pie

Crisp filo pastry contrasts well with the soft filling in this pie recipe. Serve hot, accompanied by boiled new potatoes and lightly steamed broccoli.

Serves 6
Preparation time:
  40 minutes
Cooking time:
  30 minutes

3 tablespoons **olive oil**
1 large **onion**, chopped
2 **garlic cloves**, chopped
600 g (1 lb 5 oz) **carrots**,
  peeled and grated
½ teaspoon **dried marjoram**
250 g (9 oz) **chestnut**
  mushrooms, sliced
200 g (7 oz) **peeled cooked**
  chestnuts, roughly
  chopped
200 g (7 oz) **cashew nuts**,
  roughly chopped
3 tablespoons chopped
  fresh **flat leaf parsley**
3 tablespoons **tomato purée**
200 g (7 oz) **cream cheese**
freshly ground **black pepper**
6 large **filo pastry sheets**
a little **milk**, for glazing

Preheat the oven to 180°C/350°F/Gas Mark 4. Place a circle of non-stick baking parchment in the base of a deep, round, 20–23 cm (8–9 inch) springform baking tin.

Heat 2 tablespoons of the olive oil in a large lidded saucepan. Gently fry the onion and garlic for 4–5 minutes to soften. Add the carrots and marjoram, reduce the heat, cover the pan and sweat the vegetables for 10 minutes, stirring occasionally. Remove from the heat and set aside to cool slightly.

Meanwhile, heat the remaining tablespoon of oil in a separate pan and sauté the mushrooms for 3–4 minutes. Add the chestnuts, cashew nuts, parsley and tomato purée along with 2 tablespoons of water. Simmer for a further 2–3 minutes.

Stir the cream cheese into the cooled carrots, and then combine the carrot mixture with the mushrooms. Season with plenty of black pepper.

Working quickly so that the filo pastry doesn't dry out, arrange four overlapping sheets of pastry across the base of the prepared tin, easing it into the sides and up over the edge of the tin. Spoon the carrot and nut mixture into the tin and level the top. Cover with the fifth sheet of filo pastry, folding as necessary, and then turn down the overhanging pieces of filo. Lightly scrunch up the last sheet of pastry and arrange it attractively over the top of the pie. Brush with a little milk to glaze.

Bake for 30 minutes until the pastry is crisp and golden. Leave to rest for a couple of minutes before removing from the tin and serving.

Tomato tarte tatin

This is a savoury tarte tatin – really an upside down tomato pie. With good-flavoured tomatoes, it makes an unusual supper or light lunch dish.

Serves 6
Preparation time:
  20 minutes
Cooking time:
  30 minutes

225 g (8 oz) **plain flour**
1 heaped teaspoon **baking powder**
salt and freshly ground **black pepper**
50 g (1¾ oz) **butter**, cubed
150 ml (5 fl oz) **semi-skimmed milk**
2 tablespoons **olive oil**
700 g (1 lb 9 oz) **heritage tomatoes**, halved or quartered if large, or other good-flavoured **vine tomatoes**
1 teaspoon chopped fresh **basil**, plus 8 fresh **basil leaves**, torn, to garnish
2 teaspoons **balsamic vinegar**

Sieve the flour and baking powder into a large bowl and season. Rub in the butter using just your fingertips. Add the milk to make a soft dough and set aside. Preheat the oven to 220°C/425°F/Gas Mark 7.

Pour the oil into a shallow, 24 cm (9½ inch) round ovenproof dish. Lay the tomatoes on the bottom of the dish, sprinkle over the chopped basil and balsamic vinegar and season.

Roll the dough out to fit over the tomatoes, put it over the top of them and tuck the edges inside the dish to seal. Cook in the oven for about 30 minutes until the crust is well risen and golden.

Remove from the oven and release the edges with a knife. Leave to cool for 4 minutes and then turn upside down on to a serving dish. Scatter over the fresh basil and serve warm.

Bramley apple pie

This recipe contains 900 g (2 lb) of fruit, which makes a big dome under the pastry crust to begin with but subsides during cooking.

Serves 4–6
Preparation time:
  25 minutes +
  30 minutes chilling
Cooking time:
  40 minutes

Pastry
40 g (1½ oz) **unsalted butter**
  or **margarine**, cubed
40 g (1½ oz) **white**
  vegetable fat, cubed
175 g (6 oz) **plain flour**

Filling
50 g (1¾ oz) **caster sugar**,
  plus about 1 teaspoon
  for sprinkling
1 rounded tablespoon
  cornflour
900 g (2 lb) **Bramley apples**,
  peeled, cored and thinly
  sliced
1 tablespoon **elderflower**
  cordial (optional)
milk, for brushing

For the pastry, rub the butter or margarine and vegetable fat into the flour until the mixture resembles fine breadcrumbs. Sprinkle over 2 tablespoons of cold water and bring it all together to form a ball of dough. Knead very gently until just smooth. Wrap in cling film and chill for 30 minutes. Preheat the oven to 190°C/375°F/Gas Mark 5.

For the filling, mix together the sugar and cornflour. Using an 850 ml (1½ pint) pie dish, layer the sliced apples with the sugar and cornflour mixture, packing the fruit down well. Pour the elderflower cordial, if using, over the top.

On a lightly floured surface, roll out the pastry to 2.5 cm (1 inch) larger than the top of the pie dish. Cut off a 2.5 cm (1 inch) strip all around the outside of the pastry. Brush the rim of the pie dish with milk and then lightly press the strip of pastry on to it. Brush the pastry strip with some more milk and lift the remaining pastry on to it, to make a lid. Pinch the edges to seal and make a decorative pattern with thumb and forefingers, or a fork. Use any leftover pastry to make decorative hearts for the edge of the lid.

Brush the top of the pie with milk and sprinkle with a little caster sugar. Using a sharp knife, make a cross in the centre to allow steam to escape. Place on a baking tray and cook on a high shelf for about 40 minutes or until the pastry is golden and the apples are soft. Serve hot or cold.

Almond plum crumbles

There is something about cooked plums that results in a fabulous base for crumbles. The almonds add an extra special touch.

Serves 6
Preparation time:
20 minutes
Cooking time:
20–25 minutes

800 g (1 lb 11 oz) **plums**, quartered and stoned
75 g (2¾ oz) **golden granulated sugar**

Crumble
115 g (4¼ oz) **plain flour**
50 g (1¾ oz) **golden granulated sugar**
50 g (1¾ oz) **unsalted butter**, cubed
50 g (1¾ oz) **ground almonds**
25 g (1 oz) **flaked almonds**

Preheat the oven to 180°C/350°F/Gas Mark 4. Grease six individual pudding basins and place on a baking tray.

Place the plums in a large saucepan with the sugar and 3 tablespoons of water. Cook for 5 minutes until just beginning to soften.

Meanwhile, for the crumble, place the flour and sugar in a large bowl. Rub in the butter until the mixture resembles fine breadcrumbs. Stir in the ground almonds and half the flaked almonds.

Divide the plums between the pudding basins and scatter the crumble mixture over the tops. Press down lightly. Sprinkle the reserved flaked almonds over the tops.

Bake the crumbles in the centre of the oven for 20–25 minutes, until the crumble is golden and the juices are beginning to bubble up over the edges. Serve hot or warm.

Variation Rhubarb, with some ground ginger rubbed into the crumble topping, would make a delicious alternative.

Poached chocolate pears

I love this combination; the pears and chocolate sauce can be prepared in advance and simply assembled before serving.

Serves 6
Preparation time:
  10 minutes
Cooking time:
  15 minutes

6 ripe **pears**
2 tablespoons fresh **lemon juice**
80 g (3 oz) **caster sugar**
1 **cinnamon stick**

Chocolate sauce
225 g (8 oz) **plain chocolate** (at least 70% cocoa solids), broken into pieces
50 g (1¾ oz) **unsalted butter**, cubed
2 tablespoons **brandy**

Peel the pears, leaving the stalks intact. Scoop out the cores from the base and then brush the pears all over with lemon juice to prevent them from browning.

Place the sugar and 300 ml (10 fl oz) of water in a large lidded saucepan and heat gently until the sugar has dissolved. Add the pears and cinnamon stick, together with any remaining lemon juice, and top up with some more water if the pears are not completely covered. Bring to the boil, lower the heat, cover with a lid and simmer for about 15 minutes, until the pears are tender.

While the pears are cooking, make the chocolate sauce. Place the chocolate, butter and 175 ml (6 fl oz) of water in a saucepan and stir over a moderate heat until the chocolate and butter have melted. Whisk so that the sauce is smooth. Allow to cool a little and then stir in the brandy.

To serve, remove the pears from the syrup with a slotted spoon, transfer to a serving dish and keep warm. Boil the syrup over a high heat until it has reduced to 60 ml (2½ fl oz). Remove the cinnamon stick and stir it into the chocolate sauce. Serve the pears with the sauce.

Blackberry apple crumble

Few people can resist a hot fruit crumble and blackberries and apples are always a popular combination.

Serves 4–6
Preparation time:
  25 minutes
Cooking time:
  30–40 minutes

675 g (1½ lb) **Bramley apples**, peeled, cored and thinly sliced
225 g (8 oz) **blackberries**
4 tablespoons **granulated sugar**

Crumble
115 g (4¼ oz) **plain flour**
115 g (4¼ oz) **ground almonds**
80 g (3 oz) **caster sugar**
175 g (6 oz) **unsalted butter**, cubed
50 g (1¾ oz) **flaked almonds**

Preheat the oven to 180°C/350°F/Gas Mark 4. Place the apples and blackberries at the bottom of a 1.2 litre (2 pint) greased ovenproof dish and sprinkle the granulated sugar over.

Combine the flour, ground almonds and caster sugar in a large mixing bowl. Add the butter and rub into the flour mixture until it resembles breadcrumbs. Fold in half the flaked almonds and spoon the mixture over the fruit. Sprinkle the remaining flaked almonds on top.

Bake in the oven for 30–40 minutes, until the crumble is golden brown.

Serve hot with custard or single cream.

Poached plums

Victoria plums are the best, available from August to September, but other varieties are almost as good. This can be prepared the day before.

Serves 4
Preparation and cooking time:
  1 hour + at least 1 hour cooling

1 wineglass fruity **red wine**
75 g (2¾ oz) **golden granulated sugar**
500 g (1 lb 2 oz) **plums**, stoned
50 g (1¾ oz) **flaked almonds**, lightly browned under the grill, to decorate

Add enough water to the wine to make it up to 600 ml (20 fl oz). Put the liquid and sugar into a large lidded saucepan, bring to the boil and simmer for 2 minutes until the sugar has dissolved.

Put in the plums one by one with a slotted spoon. They need to be in a single layer and completely covered with the liquid.

Bring back to the boil, cover and simmer for 3–4 minutes for Victoria plums and a little longer for larger, harder varieties. Turn off the heat and leave the plums in the juice (still covered) for 30 minutes.

Remove the plums with a slotted spoon. Boil the juice to reduce by half, pour over the plums and leave to cool for at least an hour, or preferably overnight.

Serve cold in a pretty glass bowl with the almonds sprinkled over at the last moment.

Elderflower peach cobbler

You don't often get cobblers these days, which is a shame as they are so delicious and satisfying. They also look impressive.

Serves 6
Preparation time:
  40 minutes
Cooking time:
  40 minutes

6 **peaches**, halved and
  stoned
115 g (4 oz) **caster sugar**,
  or to taste
a knob of **unsalted butter**
2–3 tablespoons
  elderflower cordial

Cobbler
225 g (8 oz) **self-raising flour**
a pinch of **salt**
100 g (3½ oz) **unsalted
  butter**, cubed
50 g (1¾ oz) **caster sugar**
1 large **egg**, beaten
4 tablespoons
  semi-skimmed milk, plus
  extra for brushing
golden granulated sugar,
  for sprinkling

Place the peaches, caster sugar and butter in a saucepan and cook over a very gentle heat until the butter has melted. Add the cordial and raise the heat a little. Bring to the boil and simmer for 1 minute. Transfer to a 1.2 litre (2 pint) greased, deep, ovenproof dish.

Preheat the oven to 200°C/400°F/Gas Mark 6.

To make the cobbler topping, sift the flour and salt into a large bowl, add the butter and rub in until the mixture resembles breadcrumbs. Stir in the sugar and add the egg and two-thirds of the milk. Bring the mixture together using a knife, adding a little more milk if needed.

Roll out the mixture on a lightly floured surface to 1 cm (½ inch) thick and cut into 4 cm (1½ inch) rounds. Arrange the scones on top of the peaches, brush with a little milk and sprinkle with the granulated sugar.

Bake for 10 minutes and then reduce the oven temperature to 180°C/350°F/Gas Mark 4. Continue to cook for another 25–30 minutes, until the scones are cooked and golden brown. Serve hot or warm, with custard or thick cream.

Baked stuffed apples

This is a traditional style dessert, but with a delicious stuffing. Serve with custard to pour over.

Serves 4
Preparation time:
  20 minutes
Cooking time:
  20 minutes

4 **cooking apples**, cored
75 g (2¾ oz) stoned **dates**, chopped
50 g (1¾ oz) **raisins**
50 g (1¾ oz) **pecan nuts**, finely chopped
2 pieces **stem ginger**, finely chopped
4 teaspoons **light muscovado sugar**
25 g (1 oz) **unsalted butter**, softened
1 tablespoon **stem ginger syrup**
1 tablespoon **clear honey**

Preheat the oven to 180ºC/350°F/Gas Mark 4. Line a baking tin with a sheet of non-stick baking parchment. Score the apples lightly around the middle and place in the baking tin.

Mix together the dates, raisins, pecans, stem ginger, sugar and butter. Pack equal amounts into the centre of the apples, pushing down well.

Stir together the stem ginger syrup and honey and spoon it over the dried fruit filling, allowing it to drizzle down inside the apples and slightly over the surface.

Add 3 tablespoons of water to the base of the baking tin and then bake for 20 minutes or until the apples feel soft when the sides are pressed gently. Serve warm.

Tip Do ensure that you have removed all the rough core and that there is sufficient space in the centre of the apples to pack in the stuffing.

Bread & butter pudding

This popular pudding is given a 'makeover' in its contents and preparation. If you prefer, make it in a large dish rather than in individual ones.

Serves 6
Preparation time:
  15 minutes +
  30 minutes soaking
Cooking time:
  30 minutes

50 g (1¾ oz) **unsalted butter**, softened
12 small slices **fruit bread**
lime marmalade
grated zest of a **lime**
300 ml (10 fl oz) **single cream**, plus extra to serve
300 ml (10 fl oz) **semi-skimmed milk**
2 large **eggs**
2 large **egg yolks**
25 g (1 oz) **granulated sugar**

Butter the fruit bread slices and then spread with lime marmalade. Cut the slices into about three pieces each. Grease and base line six ramekin dishes. Layer the bread in the dishes.

Whisk together the lime zest, cream, milk, eggs, egg yolks and sugar and strain through a sieve into a jug. Pour the custard over the bread and leave to soak for 30 minutes. Preheat the oven to 180°C/350°F/Gas Mark 4.

Bake for about 30 minutes, until the custard has set. Allow to cool a little.

Meanwhile, heat 1–2 tablespoons of the marmalade and sieve to remove any peel.

Run a knife around the edges of the puddings to loosen and invert into the centre of serving plates. Remove any lining paper and brush the tops with the marmalade glaze. Serve with single cream.

Blackcurrant almond torte

This torte is a cross between a crumble and a shortcake. You can vary the fruit according to taste and availability.

Serves 6–8
Preparation time:
 25 minutes
Cooking time:
 30–40 minutes

150 g (5½ oz) **plain flour**
1 teaspoon **ground cinnamon**
150 g (5½ oz) **caster sugar**
100 g (3½ oz) **ground almonds**
50 g (1¾ oz) **ground rice**
175 g (6 oz) **unsalted butter**, cubed
3 **eggs**, lightly beaten
300 g (10½ oz) **blackcurrants**, fresh or frozen

To serve
icing sugar, sifted
clotted cream

Preheat the oven to 180°C/350°F/Gas Mark 4. Butter the base and sides of a 23 cm (9 inch) springform or loose-bottomed tin and line the sides with non-stick baking parchment or greased greaseproof paper.

Sift the flour and cinnamon together into a large bowl and then stir in the caster sugar, ground almonds and ground rice. Add the butter and rub into the flour mixture until it resembles breadcrumbs. Pour in the eggs and mix together until there are no dry ingredients, being careful not to overmix.

Spread just over half the mixture over the base of the prepared tin. Sprinkle on the blackcurrants and then dot with tablespoons of the remaining mixture. Use a palette knife to spread the mixture to cover the blackcurrants (don't worry if some are still visible though).

Bake for 30–40 minutes, or until it is golden brown and firm to the touch. Leave to cool for 10 minutes before removig from the tin. Dust with icing sugar and serve with a dollop of clotted cream.

Tip If you are using frozen fruit, there is no need to thaw it beforehand.

Lemon meringue tarts

This version of lemon meringue pie takes advantage of convenience foods but tastes totally homemade. Serve with fresh raspberries.

Serves 6
Preparation time:
  15 minutes
Cooking time:
  35–40 minutes

6 **ready-made sweet pastry cases**
6 tablespoons good-quality **lemon curd**
grated zest of 2 **lemons**
juice of a **lemon**
2 large **egg yolks**
3 large **egg whites**
125 g (4½ oz) **caster sugar**

Preheat the oven to 150°C/300°F/Gas Mark 2. Place the pastry cases on a baking tray.

Put the lemon curd, lemon zest, lemon juice and egg yolks in a bowl and mix until all the ingredients are combined. Divide the mixture between the pastry cases.

In a separate large clean bowl, whisk the egg whites until they are stiff and then add the sugar, a teaspoon at a time, while continuing to whisk. Spoon the mixture into a large piping bag fitted with a large star nozzle.

Pipe the meringue on to the lemon filling, starting with the edges and finishing with a peak in the centre (you could simply spoon the meringue on top and 'fluff' into a peak with a palette knife).

Bake in the oven for 35–40 minutes, until the meringue is crisp and golden brown. Serve warm or cold.

Mango & lime syllabub

Mangoes have a natural affinity with limes. However, vary the fruit to suit your tastes. Serve with crisp dessert biscuits.

Serves 4–6
Preparation time:
  20 minutes + at least
  30 minutes chilling

grated zest and juice of
  2 **limes**
2 tablespoons **sherry**
2 tablespoons **brandy**
2 tablespoons **icing sugar**
2 large ripe **mangoes**,
  peeled and stoned, or
  2 × 425 g cans **mango
  slices**, drained
230 ml (8 fl oz) **double cream**

Mix the lime zest and juice into the sherry, brandy and sugar and set aside.

Put the mango flesh into a food processor and blend to make a purée. Divide the purée between tall serving glasses and place in the fridge to chill.

Place the cream in a bowl and strain the brandy mixture over it, discarding the zest.

Whisk it until soft peaks form (be careful not to over whisk as the mixture will continue to thicken in the fridge). Spoon or pipe over the mango purée. Cover with cling film and return to the fridge for at least 30 minutes or until ready to serve.

Tip You could create a mango and lime ice cream by folding the mango purée into the syllabub mixture and freezing – there is no need to beat the mixture while it is freezing.

Apricot & brandy trifle

Thankfully, trifles have regained their popularity. You can cheat a little in this recipe by using ready-made custard.

Serves 6–8
Preparation time:
  40 minutes + 2 hours chilling

24 ready-to-eat **dried apricots**
150 ml (5 fl oz) fresh **orange juice**
5 tablespoons **brandy**
1 packet **trifle sponges**
apricot conserve
500 g carton **ready-made custard**
300 ml (10 fl oz) **whipping cream**, whipped

To decorate
toasted flaked almonds
ready-to-eat **dried apricots**, chopped

Place the apricots and orange juice in a small lidded saucepan, bring to the boil and simmer very gently, covered, for 15–20 minutes, until very tender. Add the brandy and allow to cool.

Split the sponges in half horizontally and spread generously with the apricot conserve. Sandwich together again and cut into cubes. Put in the base of a glass trifle bowl and spoon the apricots and all the orange and brandy juices on top. Pour the custard on top and level the surface.

Spread two-thirds of the cream over the custard and spoon the remainder into a piping bag fitted with a star nozzle. Sprinkle the surface with the flaked almonds. Pipe cream rosettes around the edges and decorate them with dried apricot pieces. Chill for a couple of hours.

Raspberry crème brûlée

This tastes as if it has been made the traditional way but takes just a few minutes. You could substitute any other soft fruit for the raspberries.

Serves 4
Preparation time:
  15 minutes + at least
  2 hours chilling

250 g (9 oz) fresh
  raspberries
250 g (9 oz) **ready-made**
  vanilla custard
250 g (9 oz) **crème fraîche**
2–3 tablespoons **caster**
  sugar

Divide the raspberries between four 200 ml (7 fl oz) flameproof dishes.

Mix together the custard and crème fraîche and then carefully spoon the mixture on to the raspberries and flatten the surface. Chill for at least 2 hours.

Sprinkle the surfaces generously with the caster sugar and caramelise using a cook's blowtorch, or put under a hot grill to caramelise. Serve straight away.

White chocolate soufflés

Most people shy away from making a hot soufflé as they think it's far too difficult. This recipe cheats a little by using ready-made custard.

Serves 6
Preparation time:
  25 minutes
Cooking time:
  15–20 minutes

25 g (1 oz) **unsalted butter**, melted
1 tablespoon **caster sugar**
500 g (1 lb 2 oz) **ready-made custard**
1 **vanilla pod**
100 g (3½ oz) **white chocolate**, melted
4 large **eggs**, separated
150 ml (5 fl oz) **double cream**, whipped
cocoa powder, sifted, to decorate

Preheat the oven to 200°C/400°F/Gas Mark 6. Place a baking tray in the oven. Brush the melted butter generously on the inside of six individual 175 ml (6 fl oz) soufflé dishes. Dust the buttered surfaces with the caster sugar.

Spoon the custard into a large bowl, split the vanilla pod lengthways and scrape the seeds into the custard. Pour in the melted white chocolate and stir to combine. Add the egg yolks, one at a time, stirring after each addition. Fold in the cream.

Whisk the egg whites in a large clean bowl until they are stiff. Fold a spoonful of the whites into the chocolate mixture using a large metal spoon to loosen it, and then fold in the remainder using a figure-of-eight action. Quickly spoon the soufflé mixture into the prepared dishes and run your little finger around the edge of the soufflés to help them rise well as they cook.

Place the dishes on the preheated tray and bake for 15–20 minutes until well risen, golden and still very slightly soft in the centre. Sprinkle with cocoa and serve immediately.

Tip You can make most of the recipe (up to the egg whites) up to about an hour in advance. The recipe can be completed just before you sit down to your main course.

Sticky mocha puddings

This version of sticky toffee pudding is very chocolatey and the butterscotch sauce complements it well. Serve with crème fraîche or vanilla ice cream.

Serves 6
Preparation time:
 40 minutes
Cooking time:
 35–40 minutes

115 g (4¼ oz) stoned **dates**, chopped

½ teaspoon **bicarbonate of soda**

1 heaped teaspoon **instant coffee granules**

50 g (1¾ oz) **unsalted butter**, softened

115 g (4¼ oz) **caster sugar**

2 **eggs**, beaten

150 g (5½ oz) **self-raising flour**

1 tablespoon **cocoa powder**

80 g (3 oz) **plain chocolate**, broken into small pieces

80 g (3 oz) **walnut pieces**

Butterscotch sauce
80 g (3 oz) **dark muscovado sugar**

80 g (3 oz) **unsalted butter**, cubed

150 ml (5 fl oz) **double cream**

Put the dates in a saucepan with 150 ml (5 fl oz) of water, the bicarbonate of soda and coffee, bring to the boil and then leave to stand for 10 minutes.

Preheat the oven to 180°C/350°F/Gas Mark 4. Place a roasting tin half filled with water in the oven. Grease and base line six 250 ml (8 fl oz) pudding moulds with discs of non-stick baking parchment or greased greaseproof paper.

Cream the butter with the sugar until light and fluffy, and then gradually beat in the eggs. Sift the flour and cocoa together and fold into the mixture. Fold in the remaining ingredients, including the dates and their soaking liquid, mix well and divide between the moulds. (It will look very wet at this stage.)

Bake for 35–40 minutes until risen and firm to the touch – you may need to cover the tops with a sheet of foil towards the end of the cooking to prevent the tops from burning.

While they are cooking, make the butterscotch sauce. Place all the ingredients in a saucepan and stir until the sugar dissolves. Bring to the boil and boil for 2–3 minutes, stirring from time to time.

To serve, run a knife around the edges of the puddings and turn out on to serving plates. Remove the paper discs. Pour the sauce over the tops and serve straight away.

Chocolate mocha mousse

A delicious and not too rich mousse, serve in pretty coffee cups and decorate with chocolate coated coffee beans for an impressive dessert.

Serves 4–6
Preparation and cooking time:
  20 minutes +
  1½–2 hours setting

100 g (3½ oz) **plain chocolate** (at least 70% cocoa solids), broken into pieces
2 tablespoons **strong coffee**
3 **eggs**, separated
250 g (9 oz) **Quark**, at room temperature
25 g (1 oz) **caster sugar**
chocolate curls, to decorate

Melt the chocolate in a small bowl over a pan of hot water. Stir in the coffee and the egg yolks and mix well. Set aside to cool slightly. In a large clean bowl, whisk the egg whites until they are stiff but not dry.

Place the Quark in a bowl and stir until smooth, adding the caster sugar. Carefully stir in the chocolate mixture until well combined. It's important that the Quark is almost at room temperature because if it is used straight from the fridge its coldness will cause the chocolate to 'set' and they will not combine smoothly.

Stir one spoonful of the egg whites into the mixture to loosen it up, and then gently fold in the rest taking care not to knock out any of the volume.

Divide the mousse between 4–6 ramekin dishes or coffee cups and place in the fridge for 1½–2 hours to set. Decorate each mousse with a few chocolate curls before serving.

Banana & apricot cake

A moist, loaf-type cake that is good in lunchboxes or for picnics. Make sure the bananas are really ripe to allow their flavour to come through.

Makes 12 slices
Preparation time:
  20 minutes + cooling
Baking time:
  45–50 minutes

100 g (3½ oz) **margarine**
100 g (3½ oz) **soft light brown sugar**
2 **eggs**, lightly beaten
75 g (2¾ oz) **walnuts**, roughly chopped
50 g (1¾ oz) ready-to-eat **dried apricots**, roughly chopped
2 **bananas**, mashed
½ teaspoon **mixed spice**
225 g (8 oz) **self-raising flour**

Preheat the oven to 180ºC/350°F/Gas Mark 4. Grease a 900 g (2 lb) loaf tin and base line with non-stick baking parchment or greased greaseproof paper.

Cream the margarine and sugar together until light and fluffy, and then gradually beat in the eggs.

Reserve a quarter of the chopped walnuts and fold the rest into the creamed mixture along with the apricots and mashed bananas. Fold in the mixed spice and flour.

Transfer the mixture to the prepared tin, level the surface and sprinkle over the reserved chopped walnuts.

Bake in the oven for 45–50 minutes until risen, golden and firm to the touch. A skewer inserted into the middle of the cake should come out clean.

Allow to cool in the tin for 5 minutes and then turn out on to a wire rack to cool completely. Cut into slices for serving.

Spiced orange teabread

This is a lovely moist teabread, full of flavour. The flavour actually improves on keeping, but wrap it in foil to keep it from drying out.

Makes 12–14 slices
Preparation time:
   10 minutes +
   overnight soaking
   + cooling
Baking time:
   1–1¼ hours

150 g (5½ oz) **sultanas**
150 g (5½ oz) **raisins**
50 g (1¾ oz) **mixed chopped peel**
grated zest and juice of an **orange**
175 g (6 oz) **soft light brown sugar**
about 200 ml (7 fl oz) hot strong **tea**
300 g (10½ oz) **self-raising wholemeal flour**
1 teaspoon **mixed spice**
1 **egg**, lightly beaten
demerara sugar, for sprinkling

Place the dried fruit, mixed peel, orange zest and sugar into a medium-sized bowl. Pour the orange juice into a measuring jug and add sufficient tea to make 300 ml (10 fl oz) of liquid. Pour this over the fruit and stir well to dissolve the sugar. Cover the bowl and leave overnight to allow the fruit to swell.

Preheat the oven to 150ºC/300°F/Gas Mark 2. Grease a 900 g (2 lb) loaf tin and base line with non-stick baking parchment or greased greaseproof paper.

Stir the flour, mixed spice and beaten egg into the fruit mixture. Mix thoroughly, and then transfer into the loaf tin and level the surface. Sprinkle the top with a little demerara sugar.

Bake in the oven for 1–1¼ hours until risen and firm to the touch. A skewer inserted into the middle of the loaf should come out clean. Leave to cool in the tin for 10 minutes, and then turn out on to a wire rack to cool completely. Cut into slices for serving.

Carrot cake

This is popular at many sandwich and coffee bars and is always a welcome ingredient in lunchboxes – for big and little people.

Makes 12 squares
Preparation and baking time: 60–65 minutes + cooling

225 g (8 oz) **self-raising flour**
1½ teaspoons **baking powder**
1 tablespoon **mixed spice**
1 teaspoon **ground ginger**
175 g (6 oz) **golden caster sugar**
3 large **eggs**, beaten
200 ml (7 fl oz) **sunflower oil**
½ teaspoon **vanilla extract**
50 g (1¾ oz) **walnut halves**, roughly chopped
225 g (8 oz) grated **carrot**
12 **walnut halves**, to decorate

Icing
175 g (6 oz) **low fat cream cheese**
25 g (1 oz) **unsalted butter**, softened
80 g (3 oz) **icing sugar**, sifted
lemon juice
vanilla extract

Preheat the oven to 180°C/350°F/Gas Mark 4. Grease a shallow 17 × 26 cm (6½ × 10½ inch) tin and line with non-stick baking parchment or greased greaseproof paper.

In a large bowl, sift together the flour, baking powder and spices. Stir in the sugar.

Make a well in the centre and add the eggs, oil and vanilla extract. Stir until smooth. Mix in the walnuts and carrot and spoon into the prepared tin. Level the surface.

Bake the cake in the centre of the oven for 40–45 minutes until a metal skewer inserted in the middle comes out clean. Allow to cool in tin for 10 minutes before turning out on to a wire rack to cool completely.

To make the icing, beat together the cream cheese and butter until smooth. Gradually add the sifted icing sugar, followed by a squeeze of lemon juice and a few drops of vanilla extract to taste.

Spread the icing evenly over the cake's surface. Mark into 12 squares and decorate each with a walnut half. Store in the fridge, covered, to prevent it from drying out.

Boston brownies

This is scrumptious example of American influence. These moist squares are packed with nuts, though you could substitute chocolate drops instead.

Makes 15
Preparation time:
 20 minutes + cooling
Baking time:
 25–30 minutes

115 g (4¼ oz) **plain chocolate** (at least 70% cocoa solids), broken into pieces

115 g (4¼ oz) **unsalted butter** or **margarine**, cubed

2 large **eggs**, beaten

1 teaspoon **vanilla extract**

100 g (3½ oz) **macadamia nuts**, chopped

50 g (1¼ oz) **plain flour**

½ teaspoon **baking powder**

Preheat the oven to 180°C/350°F/Gas Mark 4. Grease and line a shallow 28 × 18 cm (11 × 7 inch) baking tin.

Melt the chocolate and butter or margarine in a bowl set over a pan of hot water. Remove from the heat, stir until smooth and then leave to cool slightly.

Whisk in the beaten eggs and vanilla extract and stir in three-quarters of the nuts. Sift together the flour and baking powder and fold in.

Pour into the prepared tin and shake to level the surface. Sprinkle the reserved nuts evenly over the top and place on the middle shelf of the oven. Bake for 25–30 minutes, until the middle is just firm (it does continue to cook slightly when taken out of the oven) and the mixture has started to come away from the edges of the tin.

Cool in tin for 10 minutes before cutting into 15 squares and transferring to a wire rack to cool completely.

Fruit loaf

A traditional fruit bread made with mixed dried fruit that tastes equally good toasted, with lots of butter.

Makes 1 × 900 g (2 lb) loaf
Preparation time: 25–30 minutes + rising + cooling
Baking time: 25–35 minutes

150 ml (5 fl oz) hand-hot **semi-skimmed milk**

25 g (1 oz) **caster sugar**, plus 1 teaspoon

15 g (½ oz) **dried yeast**

450 g (1 lb) **strong white flour**

1 teaspoon **salt**

25 g (1 oz) **margarine**

175 g (6 oz) **mixed dried fruit**

Mix together 150 ml (5 fl oz) of hand-hot water with the milk and dissolve the teaspoon of sugar in the liquid. Sprinkle in the yeast and stir to mix. Leave in a warm place for 10–15 minutes, until frothy.

Sift the flour and salt into a bowl, rub in the margarine and add the remaining sugar. Stir in the dried fruit. Add the yeast mixture and mix to form a soft dough.

Knead the dough on a lightly floured surface until smooth and elastic. Place in a clean, greased bowl, cover and leave to rise until doubled in size (the time will depend on the warmth of your room).

Turn out the dough on to a lightly floured surface, knock back and knead again. Shape and place in a 900 g (2 lb) greased loaf tin. Cover and leave to prove for 30 minutes. Preheat the oven to 200°C/400°F/Gas Mark 6.

Bake the loaf for 25–35 minutes, until golden and hollow-sounding when tapped on the base. Transfer to a wire rack to cool.

Blueberry friands

These are very easy to make as they only require mixing, so why not let the children have a go – they are the next generation of cooks after all.

Makes 12
Preparation time:
  20 minutes + cooling
Baking time:
  25–30 minutes

80 g (3 oz) **unsalted butter** or **margarine**
225 g (8 oz) **plain flour**
2 teaspoons **baking powder**
½ teaspoon **bicarbonate of soda**
115 g (4¼ oz) **golden granulated sugar**, plus 2 teaspoons for sprinkling
225 ml (8 fl oz) **natural bio yogurt**
1 large **egg**, beaten
½ teaspoon **vanilla extract**
175 g (6 oz) **blueberries**, washed and dried

Preheat the oven to 180°C/350°F/Gas Mark 4. Set out 12 paper muffin cases in a muffin tin or grease the holes and base line with non-stick baking parchment or greased greaseproof paper.

Melt the butter or margarine and allow to cool slightly. Sift the flour, baking powder and bicarbonate of soda into a large bowl. Stir in the sugar.

Make a well in the centre of the dry ingredients and add the melted butter, yogurt, beaten egg and vanilla extract. Stir to just combine. The mixture will look lumpy – this is fine – over mixing will make the friands heavy and tough.

Carefully fold in the blueberries, taking care not to break them up. Divide between the muffin cases or holes and sprinkle a little sugar over the top of each.

Bake in the centre of the oven for 25–30 minutes, until the friands are risen and crisp on the top. Cover with foil towards the end if they are browning too much. Turn out on a wire rack to cool or eat warm.

Chelsea buns

A traditional recipe for this sweet bun. A real old English favourite filled with jewel-like mixed fruit.

Makes 12
Preparation and baking time:
50–60 minutes + rising + cooling

2 teaspoons **dried yeast**
½ teaspoon **caster sugar**
5 tablespoons hand-hot **semi-skimmed milk**
50 g (1¾ oz) **strong white flour**

Dough
175 g (6 oz) **strong white flour**
½ teaspoon **salt**
25 g (1 oz) **caster sugar**
25 g (1 oz) **margarine**
1 **egg**, beaten

Filling
25 g (1 oz) **unsalted butter**, melted
115 g (4¼ oz) **mixed dried fruit**
50 g (1¾ oz) **light muscovado sugar**
½ teaspoon **ground cinnamon**

To make the yeast batter, place the yeast and sugar in a small jug. Stir in the milk and leave for 5 minutes. Stir in the flour and leave in a warm place until frothy (about 15–20 minutes).

To make the dough, sift together the flour and salt and mix in the sugar. Rub in the margarine. Stir in the egg and the yeast batter and mix to give a soft dough.

Turn out on to a lightly floured surface and knead for 8–10 minutes, until the dough is smooth, elastic and no longer sticky. Place the dough in a clean, greased bowl, cover and leave to rise until doubled in size (the time will depend on the warmth of your room).

Transfer the risen dough to a lightly floured surface and knock back and knead. Roll the dough into a rectangle 30 × 23 cm (12 × 9 inches). Brush the surface with the melted butter and sprinkle with the fruit, sugar and cinnamon.

Roll up the dough like a Swiss roll, starting at the longest side. Cut into 12 equal pieces and place in a 17 × 26 cm (6½ × 10½ inch) greased tin, cut-side down. Cover with greased cling film and leave to prove for about 30 minutes until well risen. Preheat the oven to 220°C/425°F/Gas Mark 7.

Bake for 20–25 minutes, until golden brown. Turn out on to a wire rack to cool.